Heroes and Saints

Also by Max L. Christensen
published by Westminster John Knox Press

*Turning Points: Stories of People
Who Made a Difference*

Heroes and Saints

*More Stories of
People Who Made a Difference*

Max L. Christensen

Westminster John Knox Press
Louisville, Kentucky

Cover design by Pamela Poll
Cover illustration: Joan of Arc at the coronation of King Charles VII in
the cathedral at Reims, July 1429. *Jean Auguste Dominique Ingres. Louvre,
Paris. Courtesy of Art Resource.*

First edition
Published by Westminster John Knox Press
Louisville, Kentucky

This book is printed on acid-free paper that meets the
American National Standards Institute Z39.48 standard. ♾

PRINTED IN THE UNITED STATES OF AMERICA
97 98 99 00 01 02 03 04 05 06 — 10 9 8 7 6 5 4 3 2 1

Library of Congress Cataloging-in-Publication Data

Christensen, Max L. (Max LeRoy), date.
Heroes and saints : more stories of people who made a difference /
Max L. Christensen. — 1st ed.
        p.   cm.
ISBN 0–664–25702–X (alk. paper)
1. Biography.   2. Heroes—Biography.   3. History—Miscellanea.
I. Title.
CT105.C43   1997
920.02—dc21   97–1588

DEDICATION

With love, this book is dedicated to our grandchildren: baby Winston Eric Searles, the brothers Justin James and Spencer Gordon Christensen, and Shelley Ann Petrie who at age five wrote to me in her childish scrawl that "love never gets breaked." St. Paul couldn't have said it better.

Also to our newest daughter-in-law, Lorna Chu Christensen, and to Winston Francis Searles, our newest son-in-law, and to the late distinguished California teacher and artist Steve Ross.

CONTENTS

Contents

Contents

Works Consulted

To list all the sources for this material, much of which has been taken from 750 newspaper columns written from 1958 to 1971, would require a library. However, the main reference volumes used are listed below.

Allen, Alexander V. G. *Christian Institutions.* New York: Charles Scribner's Sons, 1916.

American Heritage. 185 vols. New York: Forbes, Inc., 1959–1991.

The Book of Days. Vols. 1 and 2. London and Edinburgh: W. & R. Chambers, Ltd., 1886.

Clark, C.P.S. *Everyman's Book of Saints.* Oxford: A. R. Mowbray & Co., 1956.

The Encyclopaedia Britannica. 29 vols. Cambridge: Cambridge University Press, 1910.

"Great Lives, Great Deeds" series. *Coronet* magazine, 1964.

Kerr, Hugh T., and John M. Mulder. *Conversions.* Grand Rapids: Wm. B. Eerdmans Publishing Co., 1983.

Lundquist, Amos. Lives That Glorify God. Rock Island, Ill.: Augustana Book Concern, 1953.

Webster's New Biographical Dictionary. Springfield, Mass.: Merriam-Webster, 1983.

In addition, the readers and editors of the *San Francisco Examiner, The Grass Valley-Nevada City Union,* and the *Lodi* (Calif.) *News Sentinel* have been very helpful in submitting ideas and information that have been useful in the writing of this book.

INTRODUCTION

Heroes and saints ride the crest of those endless waves of change we call history. They were a part of our present lifestream, the force that ties all of humankind together from age to age to age. They were challenging and leading people from the time of the building of ancient pyramids to the construction of shopping malls today.

This book of brief biographical sketches is a collage of true stories about people, ranging from a teenaged religious reformer, to a borderline punk at prayer who brought peace to millions of souls, to a deaf and mute half-animal child who finally taught others to see and hear and speak with their souls. All together, they are the crown-worthy, the worthy, and the absolutely necessary.

The people I write about have one thing in common: they are not easy to stereotype. One woman threw a billiard ball at a bartender, knocking him out; another in a different time was burned at the stake because of her dream. They are not footnotes of history for trivia buffs; they are the very makings of history. As I stated in my first volume, *Turning Points,* we speak of people who, in key moments combining crisis and insight, found the grace and strength to change our world for the better, forever. These moments show the force of the adventuring, irrepressible human spirit as it moves in the arts and sciences, in politics and social movements, in business and religion and private prayer.

The tales of hero-souls I mention here are not the sort that have George Washington chopping down a cherry tree and then confessing to his father: "I cannot tell a lie. I did it." (Actually, this never happened at all. Parson Weems, a clergyman, invented the tale.) And there was Barbara Frietchie, who never waved the flag over "this old gray head," and there was the apple that William Tell never shot, and the ride that Paul Revere never finished. By contrast, what follows here are events born of what Winston Churchill would call "blood, sweat, and tears," events of deep meaning, events of the heart and soul that have had blessed consequences.

I should, and at some future time will most certainly, add many other names to our honor roll: Mother Teresa, Eleanor Roosevelt, Rosa Parks, the Reverend Nicholas Copernicus, the astronomer—and Archbishop Thomas Cranmer, England's spiritual and literary giant of the Reformation period who was burned at the stake in Oxford in 1556, as were two of his colleagues, bishops Hugh Latimer and Nicholas Ridley in 1555. Fuller comment on these and many other individuals must await appropriate comment in another book.

PART I

Heroes of Old

THE TEENAGED REFORMER

King Akhenaton

Great religious concepts, history shows us, are usually slow in forming themselves in the mind of man. They appear first in primitive cultures as tiny seed thoughts hidden away under many hard layers of superstition and ignorance. Then, in a process that sometimes takes thousands of years, the softening rains of knowledge and wisdom wear away at the restrictive crusts, the idea springs forth and grows—and finally matures.

One remarkable exception to this "rule of growth" took place in Egypt more than thirty-three hundred years ago when a wonderfully fine insight concerning the nature of God was conceived, born, and brought into full bloom almost within the space of one man's lifetime. The man was Amenhotep IV, a young king, or pharaoh, whose reign began at a time when the people of his country were worshiping a multitude of gods and idols. Among the many deities was the powerful Amon, who claimed the loyalty of members of the ruling class, but there was a host of other smaller gods who "controlled" such varied things as rain, happiness in marriage, work contracts, harvests, health. The practice of magic was inseparable from worship. The gods were regarded by their followers as having no authority or power outside a particular sphere of influence, and most citizens were devoted to several different ones.

The young pharaoh, according to many scholars, was brought up and trained in the worship of the sun god. In the course of time he became convinced that there was but one god—the sun—the source of all life, of all creation, and of all growth and activity. Monotheism, the worship of one god, was an extremely radical idea and met, of course, with much resistance. The young ruler persisted in this thinking, however, and in due course he began to view the new god he called Aton as the primary source of all ethical and moral being, and as a power within. These thoughts, which represent as careful a monotheism as one would find in religious writings many years later, provide the basis for what was perhaps one of the most thoroughgoing revolutions and reformations of religion in history. Amenhotep, who was named after the old god, changed his name to Akhenaton, which means "pious to Aton." He built a new city to honor Aton, he forbade the worship of all other deities, and he went so far as to obliterate the names of other gods from the tombs (including his own father's) and temples of all Egypt.

But Egypt was not yet ready for the concept of one god. After a reign of only seventeen years the young reformer-king died, quite possibly a martyr. And within a few decades of the time he started, Akhenaton's spiritual blossom was crushed—the old gods were restored to their places of authority, markings on the temples and tombs were changed again, and it was almost as if Akhenaton had never lived.

Almost—but not quite. The writings of Akhenaton, or Ikhnaton, who reigned from about 1375 to 1358 B.C., still serve as an inspiration for the rising, questing soul of man. These thoughts, for example, from a psalm the perceptive teenager wrote, will be treasured always:

> Manifold are Thy works, One and Only God,
> Whose power none other possesseth;
> The whole earth Thou hast created
> According to Thine own understanding . . .
> Thou art He who art in my soul;
> Thou art the life of life;
> Through Thee men live.

THE WISDOM TREE

Gautama Buddha

A young prince, an old man, a sick man, a corpse, a monk, a sorrowful parting from wife and child, a painful six-year quest, a long moment of illumination, and nearly a half century of teaching—these are the curiously mixed elements that played a part in the founding of one of the world's principal religions: Buddhism. One of the many and varying ancient traditions that surround this important religion tells us that at the birth of a certain Prince Gautama in India in about the year 563 B.C., a prophecy was made that he would one day see four things: an old man, a sick man, a dead man, and a monk. At the sight of these things, the prophecy said, the prince would realize the impermanence of all earthy things and forsake his home in order to take refuge in the forest for solitary meditation.

The tradition goes on to say that the prophecy was fulfilled in a literal way; but whatever the truth of this may be, it is certain that as the prince reached manhood he became increasingly distressed at the worldliness of the society in which he lived. When his first child, a son, was born he realized that his love for the infant would soon grow so strong as to prevent him from undertaking the monastic quest for inner peace. Sadly then, he retreated to the forest where for six years he practiced a discipline of fasting that nearly resulted in his death. Sometime later, having decided that self-starvation was not the way to wisdom, he seated himself under a pipal tree and there, after several hours had passed by, fell into a trance in which he experienced a blissful illumination. All the problems that had plagued him were suddenly resolved, and the whole plan and order of the life of man became clear.

After the experience he arose from his place under the tree (later called the Bo Tree, or Tree of Knowledge) and announced that he would henceforth be called not only Buddha, "The Enlightened One," but also Tathagata, "The Perfect One." Fellow monks who had scorned him for deserting the rigorous path of knowledge quickly fell under his sway, and for forty-five years—until he died at the age of eighty—the warmhearted teacher traveled the valley of the Ganges preaching his message of "moderation" and the "middle way." Converts were soon numbered in the thousands. The happy Buddha's appeal was strong in two ways. First of all, as a person he was profoundly compassionate, humble, and wise. Second, as a teacher, he held that in order to achieve illumination, each man must work out his own salvation by finding the proper balance between self-denial and self-indulgence. He taught the virtues of kindness and love, of moderation and consideration. The Golden Rule was a central precept of his ethical system. He was silent on the subject of God, and condemned ritualistic practices.

The highest state of being, nirvana, would be reached, he said, with the death of passion and hatred and illusion within the heart. This blessed spiritual emancipation would mean freedom from the necessity of future transmigrations of the soul (reentry of the soul into the world in another form of life, human or animal).

It has been estimated that more than half the world's population has been directly affected by the young prince who lived out a prophecy, who searched for and found his prize of peace—and returned from the forest to share it.

And now, brethren, I take my leave of you; all the constituents of being are transitory; work out your salvation with diligence.—The last words of Gautama Buddha

THE RANGE BOSS

Confucius

Save for one important difference, it was the old, familiar story. These things were the same: cattlemen and sheepmen were at each other's throats in desperate battle, range wars raged as boundary lines moved with the moon, rustlers were on the prowl, and raiding bands looted and burned and destroyed. Behind the violence and chaos a new social order was in the torment of birth. The great landholders had been veritable lords of their separate domains, but now their authority was threatened and they looked, without much hope of relief, to a shaky central government.

The one different element was this: a man. He was a young school principal with a hard-to-pronounce name. Everyone respected his uncommon wisdom and his skill in handling people. As a youth of fifteen he had been a serious student of the history and literature of his people, specializing in the writings of wise men of his country. At twenty-two he founded his school, and the sons of several important families were enrolled there. He accepted appointment as Superintendent of Ranges and Herds, and immediately called a general meeting. It was a long session, but no one left before it was over. Heads cooled and minds became sensitive to calm reason as he summed up his address in these words: "What you do not wish done to yourself, do not do to others." It was here that history reached a turning point.

He was not the first man to teach this principle, but he was one of the earliest. He spent the remainder of his life traveling through the various states teaching, settling disputes, and collecting bits of wisdom and ethical philosophy from the past. The writings were

7

incorporated in five books that are now considered to be holy writ by almost one-fourth of the people on this earth, those who follow his teachings.

There are just one or two other details to be added. The story took place not in the "Old West," but in the Ancient East (China, to be exact). The crumbling government was the Chou Dynasty. The great teacher died about 479 years before Christ, and the hard-to-pronounce name was Ch'iu, later known as K'ung Fu-tse, and more commonly known now as Confucius.

THE DEATH OF A GADFLY

Socrates

I t was sunset—both for the day and for the life—and the shaggy-headed old man who had the honor of being appointed his own executioner made ready to raise the cup of poison to his lips. The jailer who had placed the deadly drink in his hands turned and left the cell in tears, and a number of the old man's friends stood quietly by, some weeping. Time and the means of escape still remained, he thought. He could disavow and recant the views and statements that had brought him to prison, or he could take advantage of the offer of his friends to arrange for escape. Either of these courses of action, however, would completely cancel out his lifework and purpose, and for a man past seventy this was unthinkable.

As to his guilt, he pondered, the testimony against him was true: he had indeed corrupted the young of the community—if challenging old gods and false and hypocritical ways was corruption. For twenty-five years he had been asking embarrassing questions of the leaders of Athens: Is justice the right of the strong? Is piety demonstrated through cruelty? Shall the small intellectual gadfly of a mighty state be killed? For he had been a gadfly—a persistent, annoying critic. The jury of some five hundred men was right—he was guilty. "God orders me to fulfill the philosopher's mission of searching into myself and other men," he had said at the trial, and nothing had happened since to change that view. The precious right of man to reason was on trial, he knew, and this was to be placed above safety and comfort.

Placing the cup to his mouth he swallowed the hemlock, then stretched himself out on the cot to die. There have been only a few more ultimately significant moments in the whole history of humankind—for seconds later the brilliant Greek philosopher Socrates (470?–399 B.C.) became the first great martyr to freedom of thought.

> Truth is within ourselves; it takes no rise
> From outward things, whate'er you may believe.
> There is an inmost center in us all
> Where truth abides in fullness; and around,
> Wall upon wall, the gross flesh hems it in; . . .
> A baffling and perverting carnal mesh
> Binds it, and makes all error; and, to *know*
> Rather consists in opening out a way
> Whence the imprisoned splendor may escape,
> Than in effecting entry for a light
> Supposed to be without.
>
> —Robert Browning

> Have you come to the Red Sea place in your life,
> When in spite of all you can do,
> There is no way out, there is no way back,
> There is no other way but through?
>
> —Author unknown

WHAT IS ISLAM?

The Legacy of the Prophet Muhammad

T he ancient religion of Islam was founded by the Arab prophet Muhammad (which means "praiseworthy" or "highly praised"), whose life span extended, approximately, from A.D. 570 to 632. Its holy books are the Qur'an and the Sunna, which contain some elements similar to those in Jewish and Christian texts. Its central dogma is "the absolute unity of God (Allah), who has predestined all things." Chief among the several groups in Islam are the Sunnites, the orthodox Arabs and Turks, and the Shiites, who live mainly in Persia [Iran]. As in all large religious communities, there are wide ranges of intensity in terms of outlook.

Some authorities believe the word "Islam" means "submission," while others translate it as "resignation" to the will of God.

The five pillars of Islam, by which believers live, are: (1) profession of faith, (2) prayer five times a day at the call of the muezzin, (3) almsgiving, (4) fasting, and (5) the pilgrimage to Mecca. In contrast to some other religions, the religion of Islam is often considered to be more severe in such matters as forgiveness, punishment, and retribution. Loyal Muslims attend mosque every Friday and try to perform the religious obligations mentioned earlier. Each mosque has a mullah, or pastor, who counsels the close-knit religious community in matters of ethics or moral behavior.

The call of the muezzin, or crier, from high atop the slender tower, or minaret, goes like this: "God is most great, God is most great. I bear witness that there is no god except God: I bear witness that Muhammad is the Apostle of God. Come ye unto prayer;

Come ye unto good. Prayer is a better thing than sleep. Come ye to the best deed. God is most great, God is most great. There is no god except God." And here is the pilgrimage prayer: "O God, I ask of thee a perfect faith, a sincere assurance, a reverent heart, a re-membering tongue, a good conduct of commendation and a true repentance, repentance before death, rest at death and forgive-ness and mercy after death, clemency at the reckoning, victory in paradise and escape from the fire. By Thy mercy, O Mighty One, O Forgiver, Lord, increase me in knowledge and join me unto the good."

Islam is a strong, worldwide religion, but it is not monolithic; it incorporates different outlooks, as do all major world religions. There is, however, a strong, central core that allows this religion to have a profound effect on its millions of believers.

The trees sing of His power, the flowers waft their perfume towards Him. He is the Lord of the pink morning, the white noon and the blue evening.—From the Qur'an, sacred book of the Muslims

THE GREATEST RABBI?

Moses Maimonides

The gifted rabbi's guidebook for the perplexed, as might have been expected, was very much admired by thoughtful Jews the world over; but it also won over impressive numbers of Christian and other non-Jewish readers as well. The interesting author's life was, in a general way, tragically similar to that of many other European Jews—harassment, persecution, then flight to a freer land for safety. After years of wandering he settled with his family in Fez, Morocco, and later moved to Cairo, where he worked for a time in the jewelry trade with his brother, David. He was attracted to the study of medicine, and his quick rise to fame in this field led to his appointment as court physician. In the safety and security of this position he was able to concentrate on rabbinic studies, and soon was recognized as the official head of the Egyptian Jewish community.

As he reached the prime of life his remarkable talents in philosophy and theology came to full bloom. One of his books in particular, *The Guide of the Perplexed,* was of great influence on later Jewish thinkers and on Christian and Arab philosophers as well. The book is considered to be one of the real turning points in the history of philosophy. In it the learned rabbi attempted to harmonize biblical and rabbinic teaching with philosophy—especially the philosophy of Aristotle (though he did not accept the latter without criticism). In his book he held that the powers of reason were limited and had to be supplemented by revelation. The treatise had a profound effect on later Christian Scholastic philosophers, Thomas Aquinas in particular, and remains one of the significant pieces of religious literature of all time.

The great rabbi, Moses Maimonides (1135–1204), was only one of a great line of Hebrew scholars who have contributed much to the world's treasury of religion. The poet Vachel Lindsay would surely include him in that ". . . endless line of splendor / These troops with Heaven for home."

O God, Thou hast formed the body of man with infinite goodness; . . . May the love of my art actuate me at all times, . . . endow me with strength of heart and mind, so that both may be ready to serve the rich and the poor, the good and the wicked, friend and enemy, and that I may never see in the patient anything else but a fellow creature in pain. . . . May I be moderate in everything except in the knowledge of this science, [there] insatiable. . . . O God, Thou hast appointed me to watch over the life and death of Thy creatures; here am I, ready for my vocation!—A prayer for doctors from the Prayer of Maimonides

Part II

Early Saints

The Saints Be Praised!

"A Quiet and Holy People"

Satirist Ambrose Bierce once described a saint as "a dead sinner revised and edited." Eric Hoffer, the longshoreman philosopher, with a similar touch of cynicism, observed that "many of the insights of the saint stem from his experience as a sinner." In a more charitable vein, Nathan Söderblom, the Swedish Lutheran theologian and archbishop, wrote that "saints are persons who make it easier for others to believe in God." And writer G. K. Chesterton defines a saint as "one who exaggerates what the world and the church have forgotten."

Many church members of our time who would be embarrassed if anyone referred to them as a saint would have felt very much out of place in the early church, for that was the term used by all Christian believers. The word "saint," of course, means "holy," and believers then invariably thought of themselves as having been sanctified or made holy through their faith. The salutation "greetings to all the saints" was commonly used in letters and conversation, and one's reaction upon hearing it was not embarrassment—or pride—but rather a profound sense of fellowship and community, along with happily mingled feelings of gratitude and humility for having been brought into a special, saving relationship with God.

The word "saint" is not now used in such a generalized way, but the relationship that it denotes continues to manifest itself in the lives of thousands on thousands of men and women in every walk of life.

One of the very oldest definitions is one of the very best. It is found in a letter from a martyr, St. Cyprian, to his friend Donatus, some seventeen hundred years ago:

> This seems a cheerful world, Donatus, when I view it from this fair garden under the shadow of the vines. But if I climb
> · some great mountain and look out over the wide lands, you know very well what I would see—brigands on the roads, pirates on the high seas, in the amphitheaters men murdering each other to please applauding crowds, under all roofs misery and selfishness. It is really a bad world, Donatus, an incredibly bad world. Yet in the midst of it I have found a quiet and holy people. They have discovered a joy which is a thousand times better than the pleasures of this sinful life. They are despised and persecuted, but they care not. These people, Donatus, are the Christians, and I am one of them.

THE PRICE TAG

St. Ignatius of Antioch

I t is said that there is a price tag on every man's soul. If Ignatius Theophorus of Antioch had a price, no one ever found out what it was, and he had some good offers. As a bishop and leader of the Christian church in its very early days he was visited by the Roman emperor Trajan, who viewed the Christian community as a small threat and a large nuisance. The emperor told Ignatius to acknowledge the authority of the Roman religion by making a simple sacrifice to its gods. For the quiet thus assured in an important part of the Empire, Trajan was willing to pay very handsomely. His offers, however, were turned down by Ignatius, who declared that the authority of Jesus Christ was that of God himself, and he was not willing to compromise it in any way.

Other tools of persuasion were at the disposal of Trajan. He ordered the bishop beaten to a point just short of death, and when he still refused to make a sacrifice, his flesh was seared by burning paper dipped in oil, and then torn by red-hot pincers. The emperor's final effort was a tad more subtle: he sentenced Ignatius to death by execution in the Coliseum in faraway Rome. During the long trip, he thought, the stubborn Christian would have plenty of time to think of some good reason why he might just as well come to terms with the official gods.

Trajan's gamble failed. Ignatius, incapable of self-betrayal, resolved to make the most of his unavoidable death. On the hurried journey to Rome he wrote the familiar Epistles, or Letters, of Ignatius, which rank near those of Paul in the New Testament in their strong effect on the thought and behavior of early Christians. In the letters he stressed doctrinal purity and discipline, and called on his fellow believers in the young church to stand fast in their confession of Christ. As he approached Rome he declared: "Men and Romans, know that I am not brought here for any crime, but for the glory of the God I worship." Minutes later the lions ripped him to pieces.

The martyrdom of St. Ignatius of Antioch is thought to have taken place on February 1, 107. Aside from the suggestion in one of his letters that he was converted to Christianity rather late in life, little is known of his personal history, and there is much argument and conjecture concerning the literature attributed to him. But one thing is certain—at a time when the purchase of one particular soul might have changed the whole course of Christian history, Ignatius proved that his was not for sale.

Teach us, good Lord, to serve Thee as Thou deservest; to give, and not to count the cost; to fight, and not to heed the wounds; to toil, and not to seek for rest; to labor, and not to ask for any reward, save that of knowing that we do Thy will; through Jesus Christ, our Lord. Amen.—Ignatius of Antioch

THE SECOND CHANCE

Polycarp, Bishop of Smyrna

The eighty-six-year-old bishop trembled slightly as he faced the powerful Roman official who was giving him one more chance to live. The bishop trembled because of age, not fear, and he ignored the shouts and curses of the angry mob that had come to demand his execution for being an "atheist" and an "enemy of the state." The place was Smyrna, a city of Asia Minor situated on the Aegean Sea, and the time was some 150 years after the birth of Christ. Bishop Polycarp of Smyrna had been for years a living symbol of the pure, unadorned Christianity of the apostles. He had been converted and taught by men who had known and walked with the Master himself; and he had stubbornly resisted the efforts of heretics within the then very small Christian church to distort and change the original gospel. He had also faced again and again the even stronger pressures brought to bear on the Christian movement by pagans and others who called the Christians atheists because they refused to worship any of the idols of the day. And they labeled Christians enemies of the state because they refused to acknowledge the lordship of Caesar.

The Roman officer had delayed the order for execution in the hope that Polycarp would decide to save his life by renouncing his religion and thus shake the faith of the many hundreds of Christians who looked to him as their chief pastor and guide. "Swear by Caesar and curse the Christ, and I will release thee," cried the officer; and Polycarp answered, "Eighty and six years have I served Him, and He hath done me no wrong; how then can I blaspheme my King who saved me?"

"I have wild beasts," said the Roman. "If thou repentest not, I will throw thee to them." And the bishop replied, "Send for them." Then the Roman proconsul threatened him with death by fire, and Polycarp answered, "Thou threatenest the fire that burns for an hour and in a little while is quenched; for thou knowest not of the fire of the judgment to come, and the fire of eternal punishment, reserved for the ungodly." This was enough for the proconsul. Within minutes, the mob gathered timber and faggots from the workshops and homes nearby, and, as Polycarp prayed, the torch was put to what became his funeral pyre.

There have been few times in history when so much depended on the faithful witness of single individuals. If people like Polycarp or Ignatius, mentioned earlier, had weakened, the Christian ideal might have been swept away in the tides of paganism, the apostolic faith and practice might have been perverted, and the Christian ideal lost to history.

The bishop, like thousands of other martyrs who have died for their beliefs, was not interested in "one more chance to live," because he had already found in the love of Christ an eternal life which, in the words of Paul, lifted him above the narrow confines of human life and death, placed him beyond the reach of principalities and powers of this world, and protected him forever against "persecution, or famine, or nakedness, or peril, or sword."

A Very Early African Saint

Cyprian, Bishop of Carthage

It was not that Cyprian, the distinguished professor of law and literature, necessarily enjoyed the life of sin to which he had so vigorously dedicated himself, it was just that he despaired of ever achieving anything better. Thus disconsolate, the highborn African intellectual leader paced slowly through the rooms of the house of his friend, Caecilius, a Christian presbyter. While living as a guest there, he had been stimulated by the many informal debates about the less than two-hundred-year-old religion followed by his host, and he had been almost tempted to believe as he browsed through the brilliant writings by another Christian, Tertullian. But as to the extravagant Christian promises of forgiveness of sin, of regeneration, and of "washing" with pure water—well, they were childish and naive in the extreme. How, he asked himself, could a man in his forties, "washed" as yet only in strong drink, break the invincible spell of lust, pride, sensuality, and ambition? How could a man who walked proudly in garments of purple and gold be content with the simple garb of these people? How could a man of wealth and influence retire to the humility and obscurity of poverty?

Cyprian knew that Caecilius prayed daily for his conversion and he knew than he had been invited to live here as a guest for no other reason than to be exposed to the atmosphere of a Christian home. The mood here was truly different, he had to admit. The children of Caecilius and his wife were bound to their parents by a love that had no fear. In all the family relationships there was an aura of peace. They believed in and practiced forgiveness—they sacrificed for each other. Perhaps, thought Cyprian, the church was just such a family of God. They wanted him to join them—but could he? For the first time in his life, Cyprian dropped all pretense of self-sufficiency, and prayed that the way to freedom could be opened to him. With some misgivings, he enrolled as a catechumen or candidate for baptism in the church at Carthage and for many days devoted himself to solemn prayer and study. As the hour for his sacramental entry into the church drew near, a mounting excitement pushed the last remaining doubts from his mind, and he emerged from the baptism speechless with joy at the transformation he had experienced. "So soon as by the breath of the Spirit I was born again . . . ," he declared, "the gates of truth were opened to me, my night was turned to day."

The change in Cyprian was thorough and lasting. He avoided ostentatious acts of self-denial which would in their way flatter the heart of a proud man, and he entered with rigorous simplicity into the new way of life. He sold his possessions and quietly put the money to sacred uses. In a matter of months he was ordained as a presbyter in the early church, and in A.D. 248 he was chosen by popular acclamation to the office of Bishop of Carthage. The Christian church in those days suffered frequent persecution, and many were forced at sword point to renounce their faith. Cyprian's great administrative and disciplinary talents helped to carry the church through the heartbreaking problems that arose when these "lapsed" members sought readmission, and history marks him now as the greatest Christian leader of his century. On September 14 in the year 258, during the bloody Valerian persecution, St. Cyprian of Carthage was beheaded while fellow believers cried out to be taken with him. He died willingly and bravely—glad at the last to exchange his life for the freedom he had found.

THE FIRST VALENTINE

St. Valentine

This is a story that begins with mating birds, bachelor soldiers of Rome in A.D. 270, suffering Christian martyrs of the same period, and an ancient pagan feast named Lupercalia—and ends with a challenge to the U.S. Postal Service to deliver hundreds of millions of Valentines.

St. Valentine was a priest of the outlawed Christian church in Rome during the days of the emperor Claudius II. Valentine, a holy and fearless man, ministered faithfully to fellow believers who had been placed in prisons, and for this he was himself taken into custody. While confined, he converted his jailer, a Roman officer named Asterius. In response, the emperor ordered that the priest be beaten and beheaded on the Flaminian Way on what is thought to be the date of February 14, 270. A church was later erected on the spot where he was killed.

Many stories, impossible either to verify or to deny, have become associated with this early Christian martyr. For example, the emperor required his soldiers to remain bachelors, feeling that married men were not suited to military life. It is said that Valentine challenged this understandably unpopular order by offering to perform secret marriage ceremonies for any soldiers who so desired. Soldiers would recognize him, he said, by a ring that he wore—a purple amethyst engraved with an image of Cupid, the pagan god of love.

And there is this to consider: mid-February had long been thought of by the ancients as the beginning of the mating season for birds, and at that time of year they observed the Feast of Lupercalia (which means, by the way, "to ward off the wolf"), as a part of purification ceremonies through which they hoped to achieve fertility of the fields, flocks, and people. Pagan youths, honoring the goddess Februata Juno, practiced a superstitious custom, lewd in its full detail, of drawing from a receptacle cards on which were written the names of girls who were to be their sweethearts for the coming year. The connection, if any, between Lupercalian "blind date" cards and modern valentine cards is not easily established. Greeting cards bearing the saint's name were not circulated until centuries later during the medieval period when he became known as the patron who brought the miracle of healing to lovers' quarrels.

Just to complicate matters, historians tell us that there are three St. Valentines mentioned in early martyrologies on the date of February 14. Our confusion deepens as we ponder questions we might have as to whether our modern valentine observance is primarily Christian in origin—or pagan, or a mixture of both—or a Christianized pagan custom which is well on its way to becoming pagan again. Whatever the truth of this may be, you can be sure that on next February 14, scholars, mail carriers, and lovers will sigh.

THE IMPORTUNATE WIDOW

St. Monica

It was the last straw, Monica told the bishop. Her unruly, plea-
sure-loving son had stretched her patience and love to the
breaking point. His brilliant mind seemed dedicated only to
the goal of bringing sorrow to her. As a youth he had taken to himself a concubine, had fathered a son in the irregular union, and had
sensuously pursued the gods of paganism with the devil's own
spirit. Now, she said, he was perverting his intellectual gifts by attacking the Christian faith, and that was too much. It was this faith
that had sustained her during the unhappy early years of her marriage to the pagan Patricius. It was this faith that had taught her to
pray for her husband's conversion. It was this faith that had
brought her joy when Patricius finally became a Christian, and it
was this faith that had kept her praying for the conversion of her
rebellious son. Now it was time, she declared, to seek the help of
a learned scholar who could argue and reason with the misguided
youth.

The bishop's answer was firm: there would be no arguing.
Speaking gently, he explained to her that her husband had been
freed from the habits of unfaithfulness and bad temper by her
good example of Christian living and by her prayers. Conversion
for the son, he said, would come also by her practice of faith rather
than by argument. As for the church, it was an anvil that had broken many hammers, and the faith would live on. "Only pray to the
Lord," he said, "go your way, for as sure as you live it is impossible
that the son of these tears should perish." Monica returned obediently to her vocation, a life of prayer, even though it seemed to
her that God refused to hear.

It was not until many years had passed that her son's stubborn antagonism began to wane. Ambrose, bishop of Milan, where they lived after leaving Africa, challenged the young man's imagination with his inspired preaching, and the day finally came on Easter of A.D. 387 when her son, Augustine, was baptized following a remarkable conversion experience. St. Monica's joy was such that when she died the following year she did not have to know that her son's incredible genius would in his later years as bishop and theologian express itself in classic and authoritative insights concerning the nature of the church and its faith. For Monica it was enough to know that her prayers, like those of the importunate widow in the New Testament, had been heard by the all-wise and loving God.

A Saint, the Son of a Saint

St. Augustine

And now follows more of the story of Monica's wayward son. He was "ashamed only of being ashamed," he had declared, and there were enough raised eyebrows around to prove he meant what he said. Even so, as a youth, he was different from the other juveniles of "The Wreckers" gang. He had a brilliant, truth-seeking mind and a natural skill in philosophy, and he could make quite a case for his pursuit of the sensuous life.

From his birthplace in Tagaste, Africa, he went to Carthage as a student of sixteen to study rhetoric. He was attracted to Bible study for a time but gave it up because the scriptures, so he said, "appeared to be unworthy when compared to the dignity of Cicero."

Cicero was not his only pleasure. The popular Persian philosophy of Mani held his interest, though not his passions, for nine years, but eventually he began to doubt its intellectual adequacy, and finally, its moral outlook. "Lord, give me chastity . . . ," he prayed, "but not yet." As mentioned earlier, his mother Monica's prayers for her son never ceased, though his behavior was such that once she hesitated before allowing him to be seated at the dinner table. The restless youth journeyed to Rome, thence to Milan, and after failing to find the answers he sought in the philosophy of skepticism nor yet in the powerful Christian preaching and friendship of Ambrose, he turned to the idealism of Plato. This afforded him ultimately only misery and pain of soul as he contemplated the vast distance between his ideals and his conduct. He was, so he wrote later, completely powerless in the face of temptation.

One day in the late summer of A.D. 386, as he tried to quiet his mind by reading, he suddenly despaired and ran out of the house.

As he stood near the garden wall he heard the voice of a child from a neighboring house say: "Take up and read." He had been studying one of the letters of Paul, and as he reached for it his eyes fell on these words: "Not in reveling and drunkenness, not in debauchery and licentiousness, not in quarreling and jealousy. Instead, put on the Lord Jesus Christ, and make no provision for the flesh, to gratify its desires" (Romans 13:13–14, NRSV). The happy peace and relief that Augustine of Hippo began to know at that high moment of awareness of God marked the beginning of one of the most profound and complete conversions in the annals of Christianity. The transformed Augustine (354–430) became a prime force in leading the ancient church.

As philosopher, theologian, bishop, and devotional writer, Augustine was the acknowledged father of much that was characteristically fine in the thought and practice of later Christianity. He masterminded a brilliant and successful defense against heresy, raised the level and quality of monastic life, and won respect as pastor and leader. Two of his works, *The City of God* and *Confessions,* are popular devotional classics to this day, and many of his other books are widely read. The "son of many tears" became the man of many blessings—blessings that pour upon us still.

THE DREAM OF JEROME

St. Jerome

The long battle against a deadly fever had left the forty-year-old lawyer, Jerome, so weakened in body and spirit that he had no strength to resist the soul-shaking dream that thrust itself again and again into his mind. The place was Antioch, in Syria. The time was centuries ago in A.D. 374. And the dream, which filled him with holy terror, was destined to bring about one of the most important events in the history of the Christian church. In the dream he watched himself die and go before the judgment throne. There, in the awesome presence of Christ, he had declared himself to be a Christian and then had trembled at the words of divine judgment: "Thou liest. . . ."

The judgment was true, he knew, for even though he had all the "right" elements in his background—a Christian home, training in Greek scholarship and law, and baptism by the pope himself—his loyalty to the faith had been scarcely more than nominal. He had thought of the Holy Scriptures as uncouth and had been preoccupied with pagan thought and ways. His brilliant intellectual gifts had been all but wasted, he concluded, and he had allowed himself to drift further and further away from God. The days of convalescence after the fever, which saw the gradual return of his health, saw also the beginning and the deepening of his resolve to dedicate his life and talents to God. In order to discipline and prepare himself for this service he lived as a desert hermit for about three years, and during that time he undertook the study of the Hebrew language as a means of occupying his restless mind. In due course, after mastering the difficult language, he returned to Antioch for ordination as priest.

In the year 382 he visited Rome, where Pope Damasus recognized his greatness as a scholar and assigned him to revise the Old Latin translation of the Bible. This study led him eventually to undertake the mammoth task of newly translating the whole of the Bible from its original languages into Latin, the universal language of learned people of the day. His early training in Greek provided him with tools for the translation of the New Testament. He retired to a monastery in Bethlehem, in the Holy Land, to work on the translation of the Old Testament from Hebrew into Latin, and he was assisted by several rabbis who lived in the vicinity. His completed work, known as the Vulgate, was subject to bitter criticism brought on because he had eliminated many cherished phrases, and it was never fully accepted in his lifetime. Some of the criticism, perhaps, was a reaction against Jerome himself, rather than his translation, for in theological debate he was often acrimonious, even abusive. Within three centuries, however, the book's excellence made it the leader among the Latin versions, a position that in revised form it holds to this day.

St. Jerome (c. 340–420) left other great literary works that are still read and valued, but his gift to millions of better understanding of the scriptures through careful translation has affected for the good the course of Christian history—and the church has been blessed by his dream.

THE CHILDREN'S VOICES

St. Patrick

Padraic's usually relaxed and happy face was firm-set and solemn now as he struggled to understand the meaning of the voices he had heard in a dream-vision. It was strange, he mused, even weird—for the voices were of unborn Irish children saying, "We pray thee, holy youth, to come and walk again among us as before." As before? he wondered. That would mean returning to a life of slavery as a swineherd in Ireland. How could that be? It was hard in some ways to look back on those days without bitterness. Far-roving Irish marauders had kidnapped him many years before, taking him away from his pleasant home and Christian family in western Britain. After six years of labor in County Mayo he had escaped and made his way to the southern coast of France, where he lived and studied now in the village of Lerins. Not all of his memories about Ireland were unpleasant, however. There were the long hours of soul-enriching solitude as he watched over his flocks in the woods of Foclut. It was there that he had looked for God, and found him; it was there that his spiritual life had begun.

Suddenly it was settled. He would answer the call of the voices and would return again as a slave—but this time as a slave of Christ, bound to serve and to save. The history of Ireland, and indeed the world, was changed that day. Padraic was ordained at age forty-three as a missionary to Ireland, and he spent the rest of his long and useful life in service to the people of that land. He was absolutely fearless in facing countless dangers in the rough heathen country. He established churches and schools, monasteries and convents, and over the years did more to elevate the spiritual life of the Irish than any other person of the time.

Many myths and legends now surround the great man, and certain facts concerning his life are obscure. It is thought that he was born in Glastonbury, England, or in Dumbarton, Scotland, around A.D. 373. If the former assumption is true, then it is a curious irony of history that England, the land that has been intensely disliked by the Irish over the years, produced for them the man who loved and served them best. It is fairly certain that his grandfather was a priest of the early Christian church, and that his father, a respected city magistrate, was a deacon. But of one thing there can be no doubt—Padraic, whom we remember as St. Patrick, heard the call from God in the voices of children.

Fifteen centuries after St. Patrick, people still find inspiration in his prayer, "The Breastplate," an excerpt from which follows:

> Christ be with me, Christ in the front,
> Christ in the rear, Christ within me,
> Christ below me, Christ above me,
> Christ on my right hand, Christ at my left,
> Christ in the fort, Christ in the chariot seat,
> Christ at the helm,
> Christ in the heart of every man who thinks of me,
> Christ in the mouth of every man who speaks to me,
> Christ in every eye that sees me,
> Christ in every ear that hears me. . . .

THE MAN
WITH THE GOLDEN MOUTH

St. John Chrysostom

J ohn's enthusiastic and affectionate followers called him "Golden-mouth," but many of his fellow clergy would have found the term "big mouth" more accurate in describing their real feelings toward him. The slight, balding, austere, one-time monk had the troublesome habit of calling a spade a spade, and his brilliant sermons attacking moral laxity in high places had caused hackles to rise on the neck of many an ecclesiastical and political leader of the day. The time was shortly before A.D. 400, and the Christian church, having survived and remained fairly steady through now-dwindling persecution for more than three centuries, was now in some places beginning to relax and enjoy itself in the warm and pleasant light of social acceptance. One of the places where some of the bishops and clergy were failing to set a good example for their people was the wealthy and important city of Constantinople. Consternation was great there when it was learned that through what was almost a political fluke, John had been appointed to the powerful office of archbishop!

Those who had most to lose in terms of profits from the sale of ecclesiastical preferment, and those whose personal morality could be judged as a not very private scandal, took refuge for a time in the slim hope that he would not accept the office—for he had turned down appointment as bishop once before. But their hope vanished when he moved into the official residence and dismissed the corps of servants whose work at countless parties had made the place a symbol of wealth and luxury. Extensive revenues that had once been spent for private pleasure were instead donated to good works such as the construction of hospitals for the poor; and the order went out for others in responsible positions to follow suit. He fired thirteen licentious bishops, as well as scores of lazy monks, and reform was the order of the day.

It was not long, of course, before a powerful and growing coalition of his enemies began to plot his dismissal. The empress Eudoxia, stinging from John's unrestrained pulpit criticism of her vain and capricious ways, prevailed on the emperor to call an ecclesiastical council that obediently deposed and banished the fearless preacher. When announcement of this action was made, the populace was moved to angry rioting. An earthquake that coincidentally occurred at the same time was interpreted by the ignorant and superstitious empress as a sign of God's anger, and John was quickly reinstated in his office.

But the list of John's enemies grew as he continued to thunder daily from the pulpit of St. Sophia Church against evils he refused to ignore. A second banishment, this time to the desert of Pityus, led to his death in the year 407 because of privations along the way. Today the memory of St. John Chrysostom's unquenchable prophetic spirit is preserved throughout Christendom through special festivals and observances. His memory is most truly exalted, however, when preachers in our time prayerfully look to his example and find in it the courage they must have to say what they feel in their hearts should be said.

Because of his eloquence, St. John Chrysostom was called "Golden-mouth," and these golden words, spoken when he was on trial for his life, are our gift from him today:

> If the waves of the sea, or the wrath of the armies rage against me, all this is of less importance to me than a spider's web. Surely the waves are many and the storms perilous, but still we fear no shipwreck, for we stand upon the Rock. The sea may rage. It will not shake the Cliff. The waves may roar. But when Jesus is present, the ship cannot be lost.
>
> Nothing earthly can impress the least fear upon me. Death? It will lead me into the embrace of eternal rest. The loss of my property? "Naked came I out of my mother's

womb, and naked shall I return thither." Exile? "The earth is the Lord's and the fullness thereof." False accusations? "Rejoice when they shall say all manner of evil against you falsely for my sake."

I saw swords and I thought of heaven. I expected death, and I thought of the resurrection. I saw sufferings here and I counted the blessings beyond. The good cause for which I fight is rich enough to comfort me. I was carried off, but that was no shame for me. There is only one thing to be ashamed of. That is sin. If even the world would shame me, that is no shame, insofar as you do not bring shame upon yourself. There is only one treason, that of one's own conscience. If you do not betray your own conscience you betray no one.

Almighty God, who hast given us grace at this time with one accord to make our common supplications unto thee; and dost promise that when two or three are gathered together in thy Name thou wilt grant their requests; Fulfil now, O Lord, the desires and petitions of thy servants, as may be most expedient for them; granting us in this world knowledge of thy truth, and in the world to come life everlasting. Amen.—A Prayer of St. Chrysostom, as it appears in the Episcopal *Book of Common Prayer* (1928)

THE WILD ONE

St. Francis of Assisi

Frenchy" was a dark-eyed, exuberant young fellow, a flashy dresser, and the undisputed leader of his teenage gang. No one in that small town on the southern slope of Mt. Subasio in Italy could equal him as a dancer or singer. He lived by the gang motto, "Wits and Fists," and was known as the town's leading prankster. Village gossips argued over his extreme generosity. Some rated him as kindly, others said he was just plain foolish. His father, a tightfisted cloth merchant, took the latter view. "What else," exclaimed Peter Bernardone, "could you say of a son who would impulsively empty his wallet for an old bum—a bum the boy himself had chased out of my store only minutes before?" Tension at home could not be resolved, it seemed, it spite of quiet peacemaking efforts by his mother. The young man went away for a time to have a try at soldiering, but the experience was disappointing. The rising turmoil within, he knew, was not simply the result of disagreement with his father.

One day the hard-to-satisfy youth was pondering the mixed-up business of his life as he knelt in the small, rustic chapel of St. Damiano, where he sometimes went to think and pray. It was then that he seemed to hear the Voice from the crucifix say, "Repair my church, which is falling into ruin." At first he interpreted the command literally and began to occupy himself with restoration of the crumbling stone walls of the old building. But on reflection, as the days and months passed, the command began to take on a broader meaning. Finally, it was clear to him that his was to be a life of service to God and the church. This decision brought ridicule from his friends and a final quarrel with his father, in which the cloth merchant publicly disowned his son. The die was cast, and Frenchy never wavered in his determination to love and serve God, and to honor all his creatures. Dressed in discarded rags and living on table scraps, he went about doing good. Now at last he was completely happy.

Slowly the ridicule of his friends turned to admiration, then to love, and finally they began to seek out the happy, humble man for counsel. Thieves and beggars, lepers and outcasts knew him well; even the birds and animals seemed to have a special trust for this man who hated nothing God had made. Moved by his example, a merchant, a lawyer, and then a priest undertook to follow his way of poverty and service. Later there were dozens and finally hundreds with him when his Franciscan Order was formally founded in 1210. We remember Frenchy or Francis Bernardone, as St. Francis of Assisi—the man who was humble in spirit, poor in things, but rich unto God.

The words of St. Francis echo in his "Canticle of the Sun" (the Matthew Arnold translation):

> Praised be my Lord God with all His creatures; and specially our brother the sun, who brings us the day, and who brings on the light; fair is he, and shining with a very great splendour;

> O Lord, he signifies to us Thee!

> Praised by my Lord for our sister, water, who is very serviceable unto us, and humble, and precious, and clean.

> Praised be my Lord for our mother the earth, the which doth sustain us and keep us, and bringeth forth diverse fruits, and flowers of many colours and grass. . . .

> Praise ye, and bless ye the Lord, and give thanks unto Him, and serve Him with great humility.

St. Francis of Assisi is remembered as one to whom the loving presence of Christ was a continuing reality. His desire to share that reality is the story of the first Christmas crèche. It was mid-December in Italy in the year 1223, and the humble Francis was troubled at the unfeeling manner in which so many people of his time celebrated Christmas. He wanted to show that the birth of Christ was not an event remote in time and space, but an experience in the here and now in human hearts. To do this he had one of his followers, John, construct a crude straw-filled manger in the quiet countryside near the city of Greccio. An ox and a donkey were tethered nearby.

On Christmas Eve the ragged founder of the now worldwide Franciscan Order led his friends to the place. In the light of torches and tapers they celebrated the Mass, or Holy Communion, at a small table placed near the manger crib. Their happy worship was preceded and followed by hymns and carols. Francis told of the King of Kings who entered the world as a lowly babe in a simple manger, like the one before them, and they were caught up in the spirit of Joy as they realized that the spirit of Christ was truly present. The custom of building a crèche (the French word for "crib") soon spread, and today it is a part of Christmas the world over. A church has been constructed over the hallowed spot at Greccio. The beautiful reality communicated so simply through the use of a rustic setting by St. Francis can be lost easily in today's preoccupation with expensive carved figures, spotlights, and canned music. Still—for those who seek it in spirit and in truth, the love-giving power is present.

There is a knotty problem yet to be untangled concerning the authorship of "The Peace Prayer of St. Francis." The only thing about this beloved and widely circulated prayer which can be said with certainty is that it was not written by St. Francis of Assisi. A distinguished Franciscan scholar, Father Ignatius Brady of the Collegio di S. Bonaventura in Italy, wrote to us some years ago to say that the prayer is unknown in any Latin collection of writings of St. Francis. There is reason to think that Cardinal Francis J. Spellman may be the author, but the cardinal has said that he came across the prayer in his seminary days. He used it in public on March 12, 1940, upon the occasion of his investiture with the sacred pallium as Archbishop of New York. Interested researchers, so far as the author knows, have been unable to find any copies of the poem bearing dates earlier than 1900. The prayer differs profoundly in style from any of the known writings of St. Francis, but it is indeed written in his spirit. Perhaps someone will be able to provide us with the correct name of the author of this lovely prayer. It may have been dedicated to St. Francis but it cannot be attributed to him.

Lord, make me an instrument of Your peace.
Where there is hatred, let me sow love;
Where there is injury, pardon;
Where there is doubt, faith;
Where there is despair, hope;
Where there is darkness, light;
And where there is sadness, joy.
O Divine Master, grant that I may not so much seek to be consoled as to console;
To be understood as to understand;
To be loved as to love;
For it is in giving that we receive;
It is in pardoning that we are pardoned;
And it is in dying that we are born to eternal life.

THE STUBBORN OX

St. Thomas Aquinas

Prison accommodations at the Castle of Roccasecca were fine, thought the young nobleman, but the rope his mother had arranged to have hanging outside the high cell window meant a welcome end to the two-year confinement ordered by his influential family. It meant something else, as well, something more important—the withdrawal of parental objection to his continuing preparation for life as a Dominican friar, the reason for his imprisonment. And the rope meant freedom of another kind, spiritual and intellectual, for millions of yet unborn souls. For the youth who left the private prison that day was Thomas Aquinas (c. 1225–1274), now called by many the most learned of the saintly and the most saintly of the learned teachers of the church.

His time at the castle had been spent mostly in Bible study, and after his escape he hastened to join one of the great teachers of his day, Albertus Magnus. At first, because of his quiet and deliberate approach to learning, his fellow students, little dreaming that he would one day be remembered as the "Angelic Doctor," called him the "Dumb Sicilian Ox," but Albertus assured them that "the day will come when the whole world will resound with his bellowing." The prophecy was soon fulfilled as Thomas rose quickly to high positions in the intellectual world. Because of his exceptional gifts, the pope and civil leaders of the day called on him for counsel, and there were few auditoriums large enough to contain the crowds that gathered to hear him speak. His literary output was enormous—he often employed as many as four secretaries at once, dictating in quick turn on four different subjects without confusion. And his greatest work, *Summa Theologiae*, is, by declaration of Pope Leo XIII, the basis of present theological instruction in the Roman Catholic Church. Saint Thomas, during the latter part of his life, attempted in the many volumes of *Summa Theologiae* to describe and define in every way the vast panorama of the Christian faith, but as he neared the end of the ninth year of writing he had a vision while celebrating Mass and refused to write any more. "I cannot," he said. "For everything I have written seems worthless beside what I have seen."

His great intellectual talents were more than exceeded by his spiritual gifts. If, when writing, the sense of inspiration left him, he would retire for prayer until his mind and spirit were again in perfect order. He refused ecclesiastical preferment, and in his personal relationships he was the very soul of generosity. He celebrated or heard one or two Masses every day, feeding his soul on mystic experience. He was teacher and scholar until the final minutes of his life, yet always a seeker. During his last weeks he was often heard quoting this line from the writings of St. Augustine: "So long as in me there is ought which is not wholly Thine, O God, suffering and sorrow will be my lot. But when I shall be Thine alone, then I shall be filled with Thee and wholly set at liberty."

THE DRUDGE

St. Catherine of Siena

The much-to-be-desired act of joining the "spiritual family" of the saintly Catherine would mean far more than the swallowing of pride, thought Lapa di Benincasa, the dyer's wife—it would mean that she was admitting to more than twenty years of maltreatment of her youngest child, and this was hard to face. She certainly had not intended to be cruel, but when you have a foolish six-year-old girl claiming divine visions of Christ you must do something to straighten her out. This "something" had included, by Lapa's own strict orders, long periods of persecution during which the child was made the family drudge. All familiar contact and pleasant communication with the twenty-three other Benincasa children had been forbidden, and every effort was made to see that not one minute of the child's life could be devoted to privacy and prayer. This treatment, which lasted for ten years, had failed to accomplish its goal because the child's face still bore the expression of glory and peace within. And instead of moving toward normalcy she had, in fact, developed the habit of going into long, ecstatic trances.

Another approach was taken when the drudge-child reached the age of sixteen. She was allowed to live in her tiny room in almost solitary confinement. There, it was noticed, she hardly ate or slept at all. She never went out of the house, except to church, and never spoke, except to make her confession to the parish priest. On her way to and from church she would often be kicked by the street urchins, and even jeered at by the friars. Everyone in the town of Siena had been surprised when the girl, at nineteen, left her life of solitude and began to minister as a Dominican tertiary to the sick and needy of the community. She was humble, yet pleasantly happy, and though for a time she remained the object of scorn, it was not long before her outpouring of selfless love brought many people, including clergy, to her side for counsel, companionship, and advice. Thus, thought Mrs. Benincasa, the child she herself had shut out of family life had drawn about her a more spiritual family—a family which she, as Catherine's mother, now wanted to join.

The desire of the mother of St. Catherine of Siena to become one of her daughter's disciples was, in due course, fulfilled; but that is really one of the minor though curious aspects of Catherine's remarkable life. During her short life (1347–1380), the young visionary became famous as a peacemaker and counselor, serving not only individuals in dispute but important political and religious leaders as well. Although she bore continually on her own body the marks of suffering and pain, she was filled with the desire to heal the angry divisions and breaches in the church she loved, and she worked ceaselessly toward that end. Though lacking in formal education, she carried on a vast correspondence, and several hundred of her letters remain today as literary and spiritual masterpieces. Her other writings also stand as still-popular classics in the world of religious literature, and through them, and through the mighty company of men and women devoted to her ways, the strong and beautiful spirit of Catherine lives on.

> All the way to heaven is heaven.
> —St. Catherine of Siena

THE SECRET

St. Joan of Arc

The open-faced French peasant girl, bearing what she claimed was a secret message from God to one she knew was rightfully king, drew her breath quickly in excitement as the doors of the ballroom swung open and members of the elegant French court at Chinon turned in silence to stare at her. Unflinching, she gazed out over the group and waited for some sign or inner direction to lead her to the dauphin (the king's eldest son) Charles, France's virtually exiled and uncrowned king whom she had never before seen. Without her knowledge, the wary dauphin had divested himself of all tokens of royal office and was standing inconspicuously among the guests.

Word of her fantastic claim to be able to save the tottering nation by means of special orders from God had preceded her, as had the curious story that voices of the saints had come to her in heavenly visions during the last several years causing her to fancy herself, at seventeen, as the military savior of France. It was almost a miracle, the dauphin had conceded, that she could survive the dangerous journey to Chinon over territory held by the powerful English armies, and he had reluctantly consented to grant her an audience; but as to any ideas she might have on the hopeless problem of relieving the besieged city of Orléans—they would listen with the same degree of hope that a drowning man would have in clutching at a straw.

There was a murmur of surprise from the crowd as the girl, dressed in the black and gray garb of a page boy, walked boldly across the room toward what she said later was a bright light and dropped on one knee before the startled dauphin. After a moment of conversation he drew her aside and listened in amazement while she told him of a prayer he had made to God many months before in secret and in silence, a prayer he had never mentioned to a living soul. In it he had questioned God concerning his real right to the throne of France, and as the peasant girl, Jeanne, described the prayer in the exact words he had used and told him of God's affirmative answer, he began to glow with new hope and courage.

In due course, a captain's commission was awarded to the girl; and, dressed in the armor of a man, she later placed herself in the thickest part of military conflict and led the successful battle to break the siege of Orléans. The nearly captive nation, heartened by her courage and virtue, shook off the shroud of discouragement and rallied in a mighty effort to drive the foreign armies from its soil. The eventual coronation of the dauphin Charles at Rheims provided a final symbol of hope and security for the French people, and their once-lost sense of destiny was regained.

In a tragic irony of history, the hardy, good-natured solider maiden we remember as Joan of Arc was burned at the stake after being captured and forced to face a politically rigged heresy trial. Belated justice has cleared her of the charges, and an admiring church has long since elevated her to sainthood. St. Joan (1412–1431) is remembered annually on May 30, as the divinely appointed savior of a nation, and as one who on that evening at Chinon changed the course of history as she delivered her secret message from God.

The Monk Who Wasn't

Ernest Temple Hargrove

The name of a certain "16-century monk" is familiar now to millions of people but, actually, he never lived; he was created by an English barrister, Ernest Temple Hargrove. With the arrival of the Christmas season each year, the monk, Fra Giovanni, becomes better known, and his creator drifts further into obscurity. This is the way Mr. Hargrove wanted it. Hargrove, born into a distinguished English family, came to the United States as a young man and spent many years in religious endeavors, particularly in the field of writing.

Before his death in 1939 Hargrove composed a Christmas greeting to a friend, writing in a literary style that gave a medieval flavor to his message. The greeting took the form of a letter from a monk to an Italian countess. According to a close friend, G.M.W. Kobbe of New York, Hargrove secured no copyright, feeling that if his greeting carried a real message there should be no impediment to its circulation. With the passage of years, the letter is now thought of as the perfect Christmas card by a great host of appreciative readers, many of whom believe that Fra Giovanni was a real person. The monk is imaginary, but the letter and message are real:

Most Noble Contessina:

I salute you. I am your friend and my love for you goes deep. There is nothing I can give you which you have not got, but there is much that, while I cannot give it, you can take.

No heaven can come to us unless our hearts find rest in it

today. Take heaven! No peace lies in the future which is not hidden in this present little instant. Take peace!

The gloom of the world is but a shadow, behind it, yet within our reach is joy. There is radiance and glory in the darkness, could we but see—and to see, we have only to look. I beseech you to look.

Life is so generous a lover, but we, judging its gifts by their coverings, cast them away as ugly or heavy or hard. Remove the covering and you will find beneath it a living splendor, woven of love, by wisdom, with power.

Welcome it, grasp it, and you touch the angel's hand that brings it to you. Everything we call a trial, a sorrow, or a duty—believe me, that angel's hand is there. Our joys too, be not content with them as joys. They, too, conceal diviner gifts.

Life is so full of meaning and purpose, so full of beauty that you will find earth but cloaks your heaven. Courage, then to claim it, that is all! But courage you have, and the knowledge that we are pilgrims together, wending through unknown country, home.

And so, at this time, I greet you, not quite as the world sends greetings, but with profound esteem and with the prayer that for you, now and forever, the day breaks and the shadows flee away.

Your servant,
Fra Giovanni

—Ernest Temple Hargrove

PART III

Reformation Era Heroes

and Their Heirs

SAINT WITHOUT A HALO:
GERMANY'S GREATEST SON

Martin Luther

I t is not easy to pinpoint the exact moment great religious movements begin, but the time of 12:00 noon, October 31, 1517, is generally accepted as the start of the Protestant Reformation. On that day a humble monk, Martin Luther, the son of a poor miner, challenged certain of what he felt were corrupt ideas and practices in the church of his day by nailing his now-famous 95 theses to the door of the village church at Wittenberg. The gesture was one more of scholarly routine than defiance, but the act was destined to shock and change the economic, political, and religious life of the entire continent. In due course there was a historic encounter between Luther and the powerful people of his time. The place was a grand and spacious audience room in the city of Worms. Present and facing him were the German emperor, members of the nobility, court officers, ecclesiastical authorities, theologians, and lawmakers. Luther, accused of heresy, stood his ground while the greatest theologians of the time argued against him. Finally, turning to the judges, he made this final statement of defense:

> Unless I am convicted by Scripture and plain reason—I do not accept the authority of popes and councils, for they have contradicted each other—my conscience is captive to the Word of God. I cannot and will not recant anything, for to go against conscience is neither right nor safe. God help me. Here I stand, I cannot do otherwise.

Luther has been called a saint without a halo—and for good reason. He was brilliant, perceptive, and gifted with unmatched talents in literature, the translation of scripture, liturgies, and music. At the same time, he was often coarse, even vulgar, and one of his contemporaries, after listening to a sermon preached in absolute candor, declared that parts of Luther's message were downright pornographic. He was, as is now generally acknowledged by today's Lutheran leaders and others, strongly anti-Semitic—a flaw in his character for which apology is now made. In sum, he rejected the stereotyped concept of saintliness and tried, as he saw things, to be both natural and honest. In 1525 he entered into an "arranged" marriage with Katharina "Katie" von Bora, a former nun who, with a dozen other nuns, had abandoned the cloisters two years earlier. Luther and his wife raised a large and happy family, and their table was blessed over the many years with hundreds of guests who delighted in the brilliant, informal conversations.

But life was never easy. Political and religious issues of the day were a source of stress, to be sure, but even in his privacy he was beset by long and bitter periods of depression that challenged his faith to the uttermost. He faced these times like a strong and stubborn warrior and in the end he never lost. Depression, he said, was his teacher. His vulnerability as a human being—parent and priest, prophet and pastor—is shown in the moments of pathos which were a part of his life as his daughter, Magdalena, age fourteen, lay dying in his arms. As a theologian and teacher he was deeply disturbed to realize that he was unable to give thanks to God for her dying. Yet as the moment of her death came, he told her that she would rise and shine like the sun. And when she was gone, his biographers say, he commented on the strangeness of knowing that although she was safe and at peace in the bosom of God he, the "wise" scholar, was lost in a sorrow too deep to express.

Here are the first lines of Luther's famous hymn, "A Mighty Fortress," written, like much of his finest work, at a time when he was coming to a victory over depression:

> A mighty bulwark is our God
> A doughty ward and weapon.
> He helps us clear from every rod
> By which we now are smitten. . . .

Luther reclaimed joyful hymnody:

I, Dr. Martin Luther, wish all lovers of the unshackled art of music, grace and peace from God the Father and from the Lord Jesus Christ! I truly desire that all Christians would love and regard as worthy the lovely gift of music, which is a precious, worthy and costly treasure given to mankind by God. . . . A person who gives this some thought and yet does not regard music as a marvelous creation of God must be a clodhopper indeed and does not deserve to be called a human being. He should be permitted to hear nothing but the braying of asses and the grunting of hogs.

Luther asides:

Never argue with the Devil. He has had five thousand years of experience. . . .

I dispute much with God and I hold Him to His promises.

On the sacrifice of Abraham: We say, "In the midst of life we die." God answers, "Nay, in the midst of death we live."

SUSTAINED BY A SENSE
OF DIVINE MISSION

John Calvin

John Calvin of France, one of the principal figures of the strife-burdened Reformation period, was described by the scholar Joseph Ernest Renan as the "most Christian man of his time." A good many others, however, have been much less enthusiastic. The warmer, friendlier climate that now exists among the various families and communions of divided Christendom may provide interested persons of today with an opportunity to attempt a calmer appraisal of his place in history. Calvin (July 10, 1509–May 27, 1564) lived during an era when important theological debates sometimes resulted in death or imprisonment (to Protestants and Catholics alike), and this fact alone should make it clear that the issues which then divided Christians are by no means forgotten. Without attempting to deal with those issues here, it may be possible to clear the atmosphere somewhat by drawing attention to some of Calvin's personal traits about which there would be little or no argument today.

He was, first of all, a man of unquestioned intellectual brilliance. Before reaching the age of twenty-five he was widely acknowledged as a fine scholar, with special talent for the law. And before he was thirty he had written the first edition of *Institutes of the Christian Religion,* a book that has had a profound effect on Protestant Christianity and is still considered authoritative by great hosts of believers. His great ability as a linguist and biblical scholar was scarcely equaled by anyone of his time. As a writer, the work he liked best, he ranks easily among the great names of literature; and because of his administrative ability he is called the "organizer of Protestantism." He was a leader in social reform and worked unceasingly for better education.

It is unfortunate that in the minds of many he is associated with a narrow and puritanical form of religious conduct. As a devout and praying man he believed that religious faith made a person free to become good in character and able to perform works that were pleasing in the sight of God. He did not believe in the reverse—that the coldhearted performance of good works would bring salvation. Nor, in his thought, was the key to heaven earned by assuming the role of a superior judge in matters pertaining to morality. As a theologian he was preoccupied with the idea of the infinite and transcendent sovereignty of God. "Man's supreme end," wrote Calvin, "is to know God, especially through the Scriptures." Later (and sometimes lesser) minds have been attracted to one single, though important, element in his teaching—predestination—and have often oversimplified, misunderstood, or distorted it.

Calvin's private character was entirely consistent with his public reputation. If he was strict with others, he was strict with himself. He was not humorless, as he has sometimes been pictured, and he was never known to desert a friend or take advantage of an enemy. A frail man, he suffered almost continuously from fever, asthma, and gout, but his strength of will was such that he was able to perform the labors of two or three lifetimes within the short span of his fifty-five years. He was acquainted with sorrow: his only child, a son, died a few days after birth, and his wife, whom he dearly loved, was for several years an invalid and died in the ninth year after their marriage.

Like many spirited giants of the past he was sustained by a sense of divine mission, and was determined at any cost to pour himself out fully in the service of God. "And so he continued," says the historian George Bancroft, "solitary and feeble, toiling for humanity, till after a life of glory he bequeathed to the world a fortune in books and furniture, in stocks and bonds, not exceeding $200, and to the world a purer Reformation, republican liberty and the kindred spirit of republican institutions."

Let our chief purpose, O God, be to glorify Thee and to enjoy Thee forever.—John Calvin

FREEDOM:
THE NECESSARY BURDEN

John Knox and Others

One of the great moments in the history of modern democratic freedoms came during an angry argument between Scotland's famous leader of the Reformation period, John Knox (1505–1572), and Mary, Queen of Scots. Knox had called the queen Jezebel and had been merciless in his criticism of her marriage to a Roman Catholic. Trembling, and weeping in anger, she cried out: "What have ye to do with my marriage? Or what are ye within this Commonwealth?" The reformer's quick answer has become a part of the language of freedom: "A Subject born within the same, Madam. And albeit I neither be earl, lord, nor baron within it, yet has God made me (how abject that ever I be in your eyes) a profitable member within the same; yea, Madam, to me it appertains no less to forewarn of such things as may hurt it, if I foresee them, than it does to any of the nobility; for both my vocation and conscience crave plainness of me."

This craving for plainness of speech, another way of describing freedom of speech, is not entirely universal. For some, most freedoms are burdens, and those who finally accept them with a due sense of responsibility understand very well Fyodor Dostoevsky's comment in *The Grand Inquisitor:* "I tell Thee that man is tormented by no greater anxiety than to find someone quickly to whom he can hand over that gift of freedom with which the ill-fated creature is born." The Israelites of ancient time were so weary of hardship in the wilderness that many were almost ready to return to slavery in Egypt in order to gain security. And the New Testament story of the forgiving father and the prodigal son describes how one young man, after wasting his fortune, came home to offer his freedom in exchange for bread.

In modern times, longshoreman and philosopher Eric Hoffer once observed that freedom is simply irksome unless a man has the will and the talent to "make something" of himself. Hoffer also pointed out that a key strength of the Nazi movement was the fully carried out promise that the Führer would do the thinking for all of Germany. Along with what is really a reluctance on the part of many to accept the freedom/responsibility challenge, one can find in every society those who are sure that the masses are not capable of using it properly. To Communist philosopher and activist Herbert Marcuse, for example, free speech should be allowed only to those who agree with "the revolution."

Man's coveted freedoms often raise more problems than they solve, but the problems they do solve are important: human growth and security. John Trenchard (1662–1723) has preserved this gem of wisdom from ancient Cato's letters:

> Without freedom of thought, there can be no such thing as Wisdom; and no such thing as Liberty without freedom of speech; which is the right of every man, as far as by it he does not hurt or control the right of another; and this is the only check it ought to suffer, and the only bounds it ought to know. This sacred privilege is so essential to free governments, that the security of property and the freedom of speech always go together; and in those wretched countries where a man cannot call his tongue his own, he can scarce call anything else his own. Whoever would overthrow the liberty of a nation must begin by subduing the freeness of speech.

John Winthrop (1588–1649), the first governor of the Massachusetts Bay Colony, delivered a sermon on shipboard just before landing. An excerpt follows:

> Now the onely way to avoyde this shipwracke and to provide for our posterity is to followe the Counsell of Micah, to doe justly, to love mercy, to walke humbly with our God. For this end, wee must be knitt together in this worke as one man,

wee must entertaine each other in brotherly Affeccion, we must be willing to abridge our selves of our superfluities, for the supply of others necessities, wee must uphold a familiar Commerce together in all meeknes, gentlenes, patience and liberality, wee must delight in each other, make others Condicions our owne, rejoyce together, mourne together, labour and suffer together soe the Lord will be our God and delight to dwell among us as his owne people and will commaund a blessing upon us in all our ways. . . .

> Therefore lett us choose life,
> that wee, and our Seede,
> may live; by obeyeing his
> voyce, and cleaving to him,
> for hee is our life, and
> our prosperity.

AN APPRENTICE SHOEMAKER
LEADS A WORLD MOVEMENT

George Fox

Young George, breathing a thankful amen to his long prayer, stood atop a low knoll on the outskirts of England's historic city of Coventry and watched as the last smoky wisps of fog vanished in the heat of the brilliant morning sun. They were like the wisps of doubt that had troubled him so desperately during the last four years of aimless wandering over England—doubts that had vanished just now as he felt his whole being illumined by what he knew with utter certainty was the indwelling presence of God. He would later say that something within him spoke: "There is one, even Jesus Christ, that can speak to thy condition," and his heart pounded with joy as he felt himself "opening" to the spirit of Christ.

The year was 1646. The man was George Fox, the son of humble and pious working-class parents. Earlier, at age nineteen, while working as a shoemaker's apprentice, he had been grieved at the difference between the way his friends professed Christianity and the way they practiced it. After being upset by their conduct during a drinking episode he had cut all old ties to journey in quest of spiritual reality. His moment of discovery four years later was the beginning of one of the most significant and interesting religious movements in modern history, the Society of Friends, which he founded.

After many days of prayerful interpretation of his mystical experience, he began to preach of "Christ as the Inner Light, directly guiding and illuminating the human soul, giving men messages and quickening them for service." His strong feelings against any form of sham or insincere formalism led him to teach an unorthodox but broadly sacramental concept of worship as the silent, simple, unadorned, "waiting upon the spirit." This strong appeal to people's mystical nature attracted many thousands of followers, and his genius for democratic organization soon bound them together in loyal groups. From the very first, their firm though strictly nonviolent views on such problems as slavery, child labor, war, alcoholism, prison reform, education of the poor, and capital punishment brought them into conflict with civil and religious authorities. By 1661 more than three thousand, including Fox, had suffered periods of imprisonment, four were hanged, and many others were ruined financially by heavy fines. During a trial in 1650, Justice Gervase Bennet became enraged at the nonhostile Fox and stormed violently against him. Fox chided the judge by saying he should "quake at the Word of the Lord," and Bennet thereupon sarcastically referred to Fox as a "quaker," a name that has clung to the society since.

The gentle leaven of Fox's "radical" Christianity has been steadily at work during the centuries that have followed. The Society of Friends has been and is a pioneer in the expression of Christianity's social conscience, and it has shown intelligent and persuasive leadership in attacking a wide range of social problems. Its members are taught to remember that reform in the world begins with reform in the individual believer, and they look back with gratitude to the day of George Fox's wonderful encounter with God.

MOTHER'S "METHOD" BLESSES MILLIONS

Susannah Wesley

Susannah, the mother of nineteen children (eight of whom had died in infancy), was, as might be expected, busily occupied with the care of her home and family. So far as her own thinking went, her purpose in life was simply to bring her children up as Christians, and in this she succeeded remarkably well. The method she chose to rear them had its effect not only on her own family circle but on a whole great family of Protestant Christians, which today is numbered in the millions.

Susannah Annesley Wesley (1669–1742) was born in Spital Yard, England, the daughter of a clergyman who had left the Church of England and become, according to his friends, the "St. Paul of the Nonconformists." At thirteen she returned to the Church of England and later married one of its clergy, the Rev. Samuel Wesley, a man of great literary talent. They settled eventually in Epworth, England, where they lived for thirty-eight years. Samuel, a fearless preacher, was in constant conflict with a powerful lawless element in the community, and life was not easy for the Wesleys. Financial problems rising from his meager salary were aggravated by his temporary imprisonment in 1705 for a small debt. The parsonage was heavily damaged twice by fire. Susannah felt a high sense of obligation for the education and spiritual growth of her children, and arranged her time so that she could have long individual sessions with each child every week. She took particular care to point out the importance of regularity, method, and balance in the life of the mind and soul. Her days were, of necessity, carefully planned to allow her a full hour for prayer every morning and evening. She was a good housekeeper, and the walls of the poorly furnished parsonage often shook with the sound of games and laughter.

In 1729 one of her sons, Charles, a student at Oxford, his mother's son, so to speak, gathered around him several earnest young men who joined him in the vow to receive the sacrament of Holy Communion every week. The methodical way in which Charles went about his studies and church life prompted one of the young men at school to dub the group "Methodists"—and in so doing he gave one of today's largest denominations its name. The Methodist Church, which grew out of the movement begun and led in the latter part of the eighteenth century by John Wesley, Charles's older brother, has been known from its beginning, and now as well, for its warmth and pious zeal, and for its emphasis on the intellectual life. Its missions and institutions are now to be found in nearly every country on the globe, and its members occupy places of responsibility in almost all American communities. Susannah Wesley gave the Methodist Church more than its name, and more than its leaders. She gave it a tradition of warmth and sincerity, of piety and industry, a tradition that will continue its blessing forever.

Whatever weakens your reason, impairs the tenderness of your conscience, obscures your sense of God, or takes off your relish for spiritual things—that is sin to you.
—Susannah Wesley

THE SMALL GIANT

John Wesley

H e was a small, frail man—only five feet, four inches in height. But on the horizon of religious history he stands as a giant. John Wesley, the founder of Methodism, was born in England on June 17, 1703, the son of a Church of England clergyman. His religious inclinations were such that when he entered Oxford University he joined the "Holy Club," a group of men whose strict, pietistic habits had been formed in protest of the low moral standards of the time. He won distinction as a poet, linguist, and classical scholar, and after additional years at the university as a teacher he was ordained to the priesthood of the Church of England.

In 1735 Wesley embarked for the colonies and worked for a time in Georgia. He was strongly identified with the High Church wing of the Church of England, later known in the United States as the Episcopal Church, and his ministry was characterized, according to his description, by a narrow view of church ceremony and discipline. He emphasized private confession, and assigned penances, and he barred from Communion those who had not been baptized by a minister of his own faith. Disappointment and frustration soon spoiled what was to have been a great adventure in the New World. On the return voyage to England he was further upset by his own conduct during a severe Atlantic storm, when he was nearly overcome by fear but encountered a group of Moravians traveling aboard the same vessel who showed a remarkable spirit of trust in God. His restless, unsatisfied spirit led him, on the evening of May 24, 1738, to a little room on Aldersgate Street in London, where Martin Luther's Preface to St. Paul's Epistle to the Romans was being read aloud. In Wesley's words,

"About a quarter before nine, while he was describing the change which God works in the heart through faith in Christ, I felt my heart strangely warmed. . . ."

Wesley turned immediately to a vigorous evangelical ministry—one that brought him into contact with people of the lower classes who had been generally neglected by the church. A typical day would see him rising at 4:00 A.M. in order to preach an hour later at the gate of a mine or factory as the men arrived for work. He averaged three sermons a day and rode fifty or sixty miles daily on horseback from one preaching station to the next. His efforts to reach the poor and unchurched brought him only criticism from the established church, and the crowds that flocked to hear him were often hostile. He was stoned and beaten many times by people who were enraged by his strong teachings against drunkenness and immorality, and by strident religionists of varying stripes.

His message, freed from what he felt were legalistic burdens of the past, was direct and plain: decency and honesty in public and private life. He taught a "methodical" approach to prayer and good works, learned, as we observed earlier, from his mother. He fought slavery (then protected by law); he gave away nearly everything he earned from the writing and sale of more than four hundred books and publications in order to combat poverty and unemployment; he worked for better prison conditions; and he established many hospitals and libraries.

Wherever he preached, local societies were formed to carry on his work. These, in the course of time, became separated from the Church of England and provided the basis of the Methodist Church, whose members now number in the millions. In spite of physical frailty, Wesley (1703–1791) exercised his ministry for more than half a century. He was indeed a small man, but he was strong enough in heart and spirit to change the direction of English Protestantism in the direction of better, more loving service to the needy children of God.

During his lifetime, Wesley reportedly traveled two hundred fifty thousand miles, mostly on horseback or in a buggy over primitive roads. He preached forty thousand sermons, wrote twenty-five massive volumes on a variety of subjects, and mastered a working knowledge of ten languages. As he grew older he reported regretfully he had to stay in bed until as late as 5:30 A.M. At the age of eighty-six he limited himself to two sermons a day.

> Do all the good you can
> By all the means you can,
> In all the ways you can,
> At all the times you can,
> To all the people you can,
> As long as ever you can.
> —John Wesley, 1777

SETTING THE RECORD STRAIGHT ABOUT "SINNERS IN THE HANDS OF AN ANGRY GOD"

Jonathan Edwards

Christians who seek a better understanding of the term "rededication" as they try to revive and strengthen their spiritual lives may find a measure of help in the diary of Jonathan Edwards, one of America's most colorful religious figures. Edwards, a Congregationalist minister, on January 12, 1723, wrote the following: "I have this day solemnly renewed my baptismal covenant and self-dedication. . . . I have been before God; and I have given myself, all that I am and have, to God; so that I am not in any respect my own. I can claim no right in myself, no right in this understanding, this will, these affections that are in me; neither have I any right to this body of any of its members; no right to this tongue, these hands or feet; no right to these senses, these ears, this smell or taste. *I have given myself clear away.*"

It is one of the oddest quirks of history that Edwards is remembered not so much for his gift of self as for one of his sermons, "Sinners in the Hands of an Angry God." The sermon, which was only one of the hundreds he preached, produced such an effect of weeping and moaning among the listeners that he was forced to stop in the midst of it and ask them to be quiet. It is now a much satirized and often ridiculed symbol of the preaching of that day, and its fame is curious because in the whole of his preaching Edwards spoke much less often of God's anger than he did of God's love. Edwards is generally thought of as a highly emotional fire-and-brimstone preacher, and this impression also bears no relation to the truth. He was a tall, slender man whose gentle expression and demeanor made him resemble more the scholar and mystic than the pulpit-pounder. His delivery was quiet and simple, and he made little use of gestures of any kind. Rather, it was his intensity and his carefully reasoned theology that held his listeners spellbound. He was stern—but more with himself than with others.

Jonathan Edwards (1703–1758), who began to write discourses on philosophy at the age of ten and who was graduated from Yale at seventeen, believed strongly in a well-ordered and well-educated clergy. He ranks high in American history as a philosopher and theologian of worldwide importance. His prominent place of leadership in America's Great Awakening, a religious revival that swept the nation, was achieved not because he pounded and screamed from the pulpit but because he studied, worked, thought, prayed, and worshiped—and because, in a moment of willed rededication, he gave himself "clear away" to God. He was a true American hero.

THE LAWYER
AND THE PRINTER

Andrew Hamilton and John Peter Zenger

T he three judges, correctly attired in powdered wigs and formal robes, leaned forward on their benches in angry surprise that hot afternoon of August 4, 1735, as a silvery-haired lawyer, bent with age, appeared in the doorway of the crowded courtroom.

The venerable personage was none other than Andrew Hamilton, the most respected and revered attorney in the American colonies. He had made the bone-wearying journey from Philadelphia to New York in order to defend a courageous printer, John Peter Zenger, a humble German immigrant who, in a publishing venture with other American patriots, had dared to print the truth about the colony's notoriously corrupt royal governor, William Cosby.

The consternation of the judges was easy to understand. Cosby had jailed Zenger and ordered him to trial for publishing "falsely libelous" statements against the government. Copies of his newspaper, *The Weekly Journal,* were publicly burned, and two prominent lawyers who had offered to defend him were disbarred. The pro-Cosby judges and prosecutor knew that Hamilton's presence could not change the law of Charles I, which made it a crime to criticize any officer of the Crown, guilty or not, but the completely unexpected appearance of the distinguished American made it clear that they would not be able to ride roughshod over the defendant as planned.

They were right. Hamilton was quick to point out that the charge of "false libels" against Zenger had to mean something in the eyes of the law. Otherwise, he said, to call the truth a libel is "a sword in the hands of a wicked king." One of the judges interrupted by shouting that a libel could be a libel even if true, and ordered the aged lawyer to be silent on this point.

Hamilton, with mock resignation, thanked the judge and bowed graciously. Then turning to the jury, he declared, "It is to you we must now appeal for witnesses to the truth of the facts we have offered and are denied the liberty to prove. . . . The question before you . . . is not the cause of a poor printer, nor of New York alone. . . . It is the cause of liberty . . . the liberty both of exposing and opposing arbitrary power by speaking and writing Truth!"

The jury, after receiving what amounted to strict instruction by the judges to disregard Hamilton's plea, filed out of the jury box and returned minutes later to cause happy shouts and cheers with the announcement: Not guilty.

In fairness to the judges it should be said that freedom of the press as we understand it today was completely unknown in that crucial period of American history, but the precious concept was born that day when a tired elderly lawyer and a stubborn printer staked their futures on the proposition that when people love and know the truth, the truth will make them free.

THE SKINNY ELF

Voltaire

French politicians said his writings were immoral and burned them; church officials said his religious philosophy was downright sinful; members of the legal profession said he was interested only in protecting criminals. In short, he was one of the most necessary men in history. The man, François Marie Arouet (1694–1778),remembered today by his pen name, Voltaire, led the fight for freedom of thought that took Europe out of the darkness of bigotry into the Age of Reason.

His break with the church, never complete from his point of view, occurred when he sat at the deathbed of a dear friend, France's most famous actress, and listened while the priest told her she must renounce her "shameful art" before receiving the sacrament. When she refused, the cleric left, and police later buried her body in an unmarked grave. The incident marked the beginning of a series of letters and essays that revealed the then-prevailing cruel spirit of orthodoxy. Said Voltaire: "The man who says to me, 'Believe as I do or God will damn you,' will presently say to me, 'Believe as I do or I will kill you.' "

The stubborn Frenchman, described by his friends as a "skinny, bright-eyed little elf," was unpopular with French officialdom during most of his life. His satirical plays were banned, his "immoral" books were burned, and he suffered imprisonment and exile. His "immoral" writings did not contain the obscene language that is used with such lack of restraint today. His crime was that he exposed and made people laugh at the weaknesses and cruelties in people who operate political systems. Authoritarian governments, he believed, cannot stand to be laughed at.

During one period of exile, while living in the Republic of

Geneva, Voltaire was shocked to realize that in European countries generally, with the notable exception of England, there were no fully written systems of law to protect people accused of crime. Judges were prosecutors, secret testimony was permitted, there were no juries, no evidence in favor of the accused was admitted, the accused was allowed no legal counsel, and confessions were wrung out by torture. Religion, politics, and law were so intermixed that church authorities could accuse, judge, and execute people who had broken ecclesiastical laws. The reform that eventually came about must be credited in large part to the dogged work of Voltaire.

His plays, poems, and philosophical essays show brilliant literary craftsmanship. They are occasionally spiteful, often mischievous, and seldom profound. They reveal his occasional inability to distinguish between pruning a branch and cutting down the tree. Though sometimes cowardly when issues were less than life and death, and though admittedly vague in certain areas of manners and morals, he was not irreligious. The sincerely stated remark "If God did not exist, it would be necessary to invent Him" is widely known and often quoted and credited to Voltaire. He built a church on his estate and, in the most conforming manner, sent to Rome for a relic for the altar. There was just one thing about him: he had to be free.

On his deathbed he sent for a priest-confessor, but waved him away when he thought he might live a bit longer (thus losing his right to be buried by a priest). His last words, dictated to his secretary, are these: "I die adoring God, loving my friends, not hating my enemies, and detesting persecution."

> "I disapprove of what you say, but I will defend to the death your right to say it." (This statement, often erroneously attributed to Voltaire, is in fact a remark by one of his biographers, S. G. Tallentyre [1906], who was trying to sum up Voltaire's philosophy.)

> O God unrecognized, whom all Thy works proclaim,
> O God, hear these my final words:
> If ever I have erred, 'twas searching for Thy law;
> My heart may go astray, but it is full of Thee.
> —Voltaire

PAINTING FOR GOD'S GLORY

Benjamin West

Members of that small Quaker meeting in Springfield, Pennsylvania, many years ago had never before been faced with such a problem. If they allowed this talented boy to grow up as an artist, who could tell what might happen? Artists, they mused, were a strange lot, and there was no doubting that the youth would be exposed to great dangers of soul. On the other hand, there was the unmistakable stamp of genius in the lad's drawings. With never a day of professional instructions he produced things of real beauty—God's beauty. What to do?

A meeting had been convened to settle the issue and they waited in silence for a "leading" of God's Spirit, as Quakers do. The solemn, bearded elders sat quietly, faces immobile, in the plain, austere meeting-house. The silence was broken then as one of the members received a leading: "Talents are gifts of God," he said, and the silence was resumed. Soon another was led: "Talent should be used for God's glory." After a time the elders exchanged glances and directed the boy to the center of the room where they gathered around him. Tenderly and prayerfully they laid their hands on him, consecrating him to the ministry of painting for God. Their action was unique in the history of Quakerism, but so were his talents, for the boy was Benjamin West (1738–1820), famed painter of historical scenes and sunsets. In later travel and work abroad he became a close personal friend of England's great painter, Sir Joshua Reynolds, succeeding him as president of Britain's Royal Academy.

The talented West, who missed obscurity by just one evening of prayer, has left us many art treasures, including *Penn's Treaty*

with the Indians, Alexander the Great and His Physicians, and
Christ Healing the Sick.

And something else has come to us from the prayerful adventuring of his parents and elders—another bright moment in the wonderfully varied history of religion in America.

Benjamin West told of another incident in his life that probably had just as much influence on his career as an artist as that special evening in the meetinghouse when he was a boy. As a very young boy he discovered some colored inks in his home and decided to paint a portrait of his little sister, Sally. He made a terrible mess of the project, spilling and splashing ink around the room. When his mother came on the scene shortly after, he was sure that he was going to be in serious trouble. His mother, viewing the disaster scene, caught her breath, leaned over and picked up the blotched paper and declared, "Why, it's Sally," and then she leaned over and kissed little Benjamin. He was often heard to say in later years that his mother's kiss of loving forgiveness and acceptance had made him a painter.

THE DECLARATION OF THE
RIGHTS OF THE CHILD

Millions of children born this year will go to bed hungry every night and they will be plagued by chronic illnesses. Most will reach adulthood, but their life spans will be far shorter than that of the average American. Many children will receive no medical attention whatsoever, enjoy no educational or recreational facilities, and have no legal protection. In the words of Elizabeth Barrett Browning, quoted in a pamphlet issued by the United Nations Children's Fund, they will be "weeping in the playtime of the others."

No generation in history has been more "rights conscious" than ours, and it is no surprise that the UN General Assembly, by unanimous vote, was moved in 1959 to make a Declaration of the Rights of the Child. Admittedly, the declaration lacks the weight of law. Its moral force is great, however, and the very act of putting humankind's hope for children into words is itself one important step in the direction of bringing this hope to reality.

Summary of the declaration: The Preamble states that the child, because of physical and mental immaturity, needs special safeguards and care, both before and after birth, and that individuals and groups should strive to achieve children's rights by legislative and other means. Humanity, it says, owes the child the best it has to give.

Then, in ten carefully worded principles, the declaration affirms that all children are entitled to

1. the enjoyment of the rights mentioned, without an exception whatsoever, regardless of race, color, sex, religion or nationality;

2. special protection, opportunities and facilities to enable them to develop in a healthy and normal manner, in freedom and dignity;

3. a name and nationality;

4. social security, including adequate nutrition, housing, recreation and medical services;

5. special treatment, education and care if handicapped;

6. love and understanding and an atmosphere of affection and security, in the care and under the responsibility of their parents whenever possible;

7. free education and recreation and equal opportunity to develop their individual abilities;

8. prompt protection and relief in times of disaster;

9. protection against all forms of neglect, cruelty and exploitation;

10. protection from any form of racial, religious or other discrimination, and an upbringing in a spirit of peace and universal brotherhood.

A COINCIDENCE?

William Holmes McGuffey

Suddenly, the young mother stopped and knelt to pray in the dusty farmyard. It was a strong prayer, earnestly made, that God would open to her some way to give her son an education. Though she prayed with great faith, she hardly would have believed that this prayer would someday mean the placing of millions of textbooks in American schools, or that the name of the boy for whom she prayed would someday stand as a bright light in early American education. Nor could the Reverend Thomas Hughes have dreamed of such a consequence as he stood quietly some distance from her, his approach to the house having been abruptly stopped by the touching sight of the woman at prayer.

When she had finished, he came on into the yard and they discussed the boy's future. Young William was a good boy, she said, with a great love for learning in general and for the Bible in particular. Mr. Hughes, by what seemed more than coincidence, was seeking students for his Washington Academy and College, and he arranged for the boy's enrollment there.

William lived up to every hope and promise. Early in life he was ordained into the Presbyterian ministry, and at the same time taught philosophy and ancient languages. He was president, in turn, of Cincinnati College and Ohio University. His special love was the education of children; and in his books for them he conveyed a rich and trusting faith in a loving God. The simple, homely virtues were for him the great virtues; and this was evident in all his books.

William Holmes McGuffey (1800–1873) was born in Pennsylvania. His famed McGuffey's Readers and Spellers were used extensively from 1836 to as late as 1920, with more than 122 million copies being printed. The name McGuffey points not just to an era but to a special quality in American education.

If we work upon marble, it will perish.
If we work upon brass, time will efface it.
If we rear temples, they will crumble to dust.
But if we work upon men's immortal minds,
If we imbue them with high principles,
With the just fear of God and love of their fellow men,
We engrave on those tablets something which no time can efface,
And which will brighten and brighten to all eternity.

—Daniel Webster, in a speech given
at Faneuil Hall, Boston, 1852

THE DEVIL'S DOCTOR?

James Simpson

Most religious leaders in Scotland a century and a half ago, together with scores of prominent physicians, joined in calling young Dr. James Simpson "an agent of the devil engaged in weird medical experiments." Their influence was great and they were able to make it frequently and painfully felt: barbs from the pulpit, criticism in religious and medical journals, and insults from the lips of strangers who passed him on the street. The good doctor, himself a believing and practicing Christian, was as a result almost tempted to abandon his daring research project.

The arguments against Dr. Simpson were simple, and, given the times, quite believable: Adam and Eve had disobeyed God in the Garden of Eden, and as punishment God had decreed that henceforth women should bear their children in pain and sorrow. The doctor was known to be experimenting with a substance that would reduce or eliminate the pains of childbirth. If he succeeded, God's will would surely be denied.

Dr. Simpson considered these arguments carefully and then went ahead with his experiments. To those who continued in opposition, he had this to say: "In the infinitude of His love to our fallen race, God offers to each of us individually a free and full pardon, and life now and forever, if we only believe in Jesus Christ, His Son, whom He sent to suffer in our stead—to die that we might live." His agility in quoting scripture didn't seem to help, however. In 1847, after earlier experiments with ether, he discovered through self-experiments the anesthetic properties of chloroform and advocated its use in surgical and obstetrical practice. Protests continued until 1853 when Queen Victoria finally silenced all opposition by making use of the anesthetic during the birth of her son, Prince Leopold.

Sir James Young Simpson (1811–1870), the seventh son of a humble baker, made many contributions to medical science, but he never felt that he had left or outgrown his religious faith. When he was asked to describe his greatest moment of discovery, he replied that it occurred when he found Jesus Christ to be his Savior. That prime discovery, with its enabling gift of uncompromising dedication, led to another that has since brought relief from suffering to millions of people throughout the world.

Bitter tensions between religion and medicine are not inevitable in the order of things. In psychiatry, where conflicts with religion often occur, there is this interesting point of view set forth by Dr. James T. Fisher, a prominent authority and author of the book *A Few Buttons Missing: The Case Book of a Psychiatrist* (Lippincott):

> If you were to take the sum total of all the authoritative articles ever written by the most qualified of psychologists and psychiatrists on the subject of mental hygiene, if you were to combine and refine them and cleave out the excess verbiage, if you were to take the whole of the meat and none of the parsley, and if you were to have these unadulterated bits of pure scientific knowledge concisely expressed by the most capable of living poets, you would have an awkward and incomplete summation of the Sermon on the Mount.

PART IV

Nineteenth-Century Notables

THE ANGRY POET

Emma Lazarus

The hands of the sensitive young Jewish poet began to tremble as she experienced a deep and savage kind of anger she had never felt before. The year was 1880, and as she read the newspaper account of czarist persecutions of Jews in Russia she found herself vowing to leave the genteel, ivory-tower life of quiet refinement and enter into battle on behalf of her people. Putting the newspaper aside, she sat in silence for several minutes thinking over ways in which she could help. For one thing, she thought, she could use her talents to rouse the Jewish people to a stronger sense of unity. And, there was the matter of her own weak loyalty to the ancient faith. Up to now she had rarely appeared at synagogue. This would change.

Poet Ralph Waldo Emerson and other close friends were astounded some months later to note the new fire and enthusiasm that began to show itself in her poems. Turning away forever from flimsy and romantic themes, she directed her now strong, prophetic voice toward the great social issues as she saw them. The national Jewish conscience was stirred; and the then-forming Zionist movement gained great impetus as she called on all Jews to share in the fulfillment of their destiny. Her relationship with the synagogue took on new meaning as she began to take a personal part in its observances. For the remainder of her short life, Emma Lazarus (1849–1887) devoted herself unstintingly to the cause of Jewish nationalism, and she is remembered today as one of the great women of her religion.

Nor is she remembered only by those of her own faith. One of her poems, "The New Colossus," dedicated to and now engraved on the Statue of Liberty, became a part of best-loved world literature almost from the day of its publication. Its lines have raised the hopes of millions of oppressed peoples throughout the world who look to this country as the stronghold of freedom; and as long as Americans keep the lines deeply engraved in their hearts, the freedom-hungry immigrants will find it here:

Not like the brazen giant of Greek fame,
With conquering limbs astride from land to land;
Here at our sea-washed, sunset gates shall stand
A mighty woman with a torch, whose flame
Is the imprisoned lightning, and her name Mother of Exiles.
From her beacon hand
Glows world-wide welcome; her mild eyes command
The air-bridged harbor that twin cities frame.
"Keep, ancient lands, your storied pomp!" cries she
With silent lips. "Give me your tired, your poor,
Your huddled masses yearning to be free,
The wretched refuse of your teeming shore.
Send these, the homeless, tempest-tossed to me.
I lift my lamp beside the golden door."

THE PRIZE

Alfred Nobel

The bright but sickly and nervous young Swede staked everything he had on the powers of nitroglycerine—and even hope itself—but he couldn't have been more of a loser. As a medicine it failed ultimately to sustain his weak heart; and as a dreadful explosive it failed to bring reality to his hope for world peace through fear. Alfred Nobel, born on October 21, 1833, was led into the study of nitroglycerine by his father, Emmanuel, an expert in the field of munitions. The substance was used then, as now, as a heart stimulant, and although it was known to have explosive properties, no one had been able to learn the secret of its control. A thimbleful of the dangerous liquid, lightly tapped, might spill harmlessly—or it might explode with force sufficient to kill everyone within a radius of many yards. Emmanuel was strongly determined to find some use for it in the munitions industry, and Alfred, caught up in the spirit of the search, became equally devoted to the task. During the course of experimentation, Alfred's younger brother was killed by an accidental explosion, and Emmanuel was so stricken with grief that his part in the research ended.

Before a decade had passed, Alfred developed what he called a "blasting oil," and he was able to prove to eager buyers that it could be exploded only by confining it in a container and then applying a sharp blow. He invented what is now called the "blasting cap" to supply this preliminary impact. Nobel's "soup" began to find wide industrial use, but it was still dangerous. One of his factories blew up, killing several people; a ship carrying the fluid exploded and nearly destroyed a harbor in Panama; and an express wagon carrying nitroglycerine in San Francisco suddenly blew up and wrecked a whole block of buildings. Nobel finally discovered (some say by accident) that when the unstable liquid was mixed with an absorbent, inert substance (like soft, porous earth), it came to resemble thick putty and could be transported easily and safely. In 1867 he patented this mixture under the name of dynamite. Nobel rejoiced for two separate reasons. First, he was certain that the terrible destructive power of dynamite would, through fear, force the nations into peace. Second, huge profits began to accumulate from his several factories and he was soon a millionaire many times over.

His remaining years were filled with bitter disappointment, however. His attempt to settle into a life of scholarly ease was spoiled by the slow-coming realization that instead of forcing peace he had simply added a newer and more terrible weapon to the arsenal of war. His extreme wealth made him suspicious of anyone who courted his affection, so he never married. His health began to fail, and it was, ironically, nitroglycerine used as a heart stimulant that kept him alive but was useless finally after a massive, fatal heart attack on December 10, 1896. Before his death, having realized the futility of peace through fear, he decided that his huge fortune should be left in trust and the proceeds from it used annually through the Nobel Peace Prize to reward someone who had distinguished himself or herself in work toward peace. Perhaps his money can do what he could not do. Time—if there is enough left—will tell.

> Would you end war?
> Create great Peace . . .
> The peace that demands all of a man,
> His love, his life, his veriest self. . . .
> —James Oppenheim,
> American poet and fiction writer

The Hatchet Job

Carry Nation

Arguments between clergyperson and spouse seldom revolve around such things as the wife's conduct in bombarding a bartender with billiard balls, but one such verbal battle—destined to leave an indelible mark on American history—did occur in Medicine Lodge, Kansas, many years ago.

It happened this way: Several days before the quarrel the minister had been embarrassed by her long prayer vigil on the front steps of a saloon which was operating in spite of the state's prohibition law. As a strong believer in total abstinence from liquor and tobacco and as one intensely devoted to the cause of prohibition, she had prayed for lightning to strike the place and, as if in partial answer to her prayer, a strong wind had arisen and nearly blown it apart. After the storm the proprietor of the illegal establishment had closed up and left the city.

Thus encouraged, the big, strapping woman had walked into a combination pool hall–saloon in the nearby town of Kiowa and, on impulse, had picked up a billiard ball and flung it at the bartender, knocking him unconscious. As the customers scrambled for safety, she had pitched all the rest of the balls and shattered every bottle in sight. She had left the battered bistro rejoicing in the realization that, if the saloons were operating illegally, there surely could be no law against wrecking them. The Reverend David Nation (her second husband) was also devoted to the prohibition cause, but he had drawn the line at this tactic. In the argument that followed the Kiowa incident, he sarcastically pointed out that she might as well have used an ax in destroying the place. She countered with the assertion that his suggestion was one of the few really sensible things that had come out of his mouth during the whole course of their marriage.

Days later she appeared in her usual somber black attire, wearing a little red hatchet in a leather shoulder holster—a kind of demolition badge. In the months that followed she became a national figure as she foraged in and out of saloons across the country, leaving a path of destruction. None could stay her hand; even John L. Sullivan, onetime world champion boxer, hid from her when she stood on the sidewalk in front of his saloon in New York and challenged him to open up his "drunkard factory." The prohibition efforts of Carry Nation (1846–1911) reached their peak in the year 1907 and thereafter fell into sharp decline. Publicity-wise saloon keepers tried to goad her into raiding their places, knowing that any damage would be more than made up for by increased business following the publicity. In a Kentucky foray she suffered the ignominy of having a chair broken over her head, and her one-woman raids on tobacco warehouses in North Carolina were pathetic, laughed-at failures.

It could be argued, perhaps, that in some ways her life was a tragic failure. She died almost penniless because she always gave the handsome lecture fees she received to help the needy. She was divorced from her second husband, David Nation, but only because she was obsessed with what was to her a great ideal. She was unable to save the life of her first husband, Dr. Charles Gloyd, but only because the alcoholism from which he died had taken its hold before their marriage. The national prohibition law for which she fought was never enacted in her lifetime, but she did more than any other individual to arouse and direct public sentiment for its eventual passage. It was repealed, of course, in a few short years. But if she was a failure, she was the strongest one in history; for, after all, how many women before or since have been able to hold off the unnumbered hosts of a thirsty male population simply by waving an ax?

THE LOST SOUL

Robert Louis Stevenson

The young man's father thought of him as a lost soul; his doctor looked at him as doomed to an early death from tuberculosis; his professors at Edinburgh labeled him a terrible speller and clumsy essayist; and his friends saw him as a frail and sickly dreamer who was thoroughly detached from the realities of this world. These judgments could not have been more mistaken. Robert Louis Stevenson's soul was not lost, only freed. His father, referred to by Stevenson as "that stormy and tender old man," was convinced that the boy was soon to die; and he felt obliged, therefore, to try to fill him with the somber and sometimes frightening religion not uncommon in the Scotland of that day. The freehearted youth's rejection of this philosophy served to temporarily blind his father to the fact that the boy had in truth achieved a remarkable largeness of soul.

The day came when one of Stevenson's books, *Dr. Jekyll and Mr. Hyde,* was quoted from nearly every pulpit in the English-speaking world as a moral allegory dramatizing the conflict of good and evil. Stevenson's personal philosophy is best described as a morality of kindness—a graceful kindness that made it possible for him on one occasion to shake hands warmly with lepers on the island of Molokai and accept without flinching a partly smoked cigarette offered to him by one of the disfigured sufferers. Kindness, he felt, was the root of all morality, and his prayers written at Vailima on the island of Samoa reveal the thought that all human happiness and peace of mind must come from this basic source.

Stevenson's doctor was only partly right about the early death, and completely wrong about the reason. The Scottish storyteller literally willed himself to live through endless bouts of consumptive bleeding and died at forty-four from a stroke, not tuberculosis. He faced death as casually as most men face an opponent in a friendly card game. No one can say now that death really won. His professors lived to apologize for their error. Dictionaries with perfect spelling are everywhere to be found, but happy, pioneering minds in the field of literature are few and far between. Shortly after college, his literary style improved and his essays and stories began to take better form. Within a few years he had developed the kind of style necessary to communicate the wonderfully imaginative tales that rushed out of his mind. He was born in 1850, and before he died on December 3, 1894, his friends had an opportunity to have second thoughts about the "dream world" in which he lived. His bouts with death were reality; he was often forced to lie perfectly still for days on end, knowing that the slightest exertion would cause fatal bleeding in his lungs. He was no armchair adventurer—his honeymoon was spent in an abandoned silver mine in California, and the story *Treasure Island* is based on his travels and adventures in the South Seas.

There are all kinds of realities. Stevenson's spirit—quick and happy and at peace with itself—found its way to the heart of reality and, through his writings, continues to lead people there today.

I refuse to let my horizon be bounded by a row of medicine bottles.—Robert Louis Stevenson

> Under the wide and starry sky,
> Dig the grave and let me lie:
> Glad did I live and gladly die,
>   And I laid me down with a will.
>
> This be the verse you grave for me:
> "Here he lies where he longed to be;
> Home is the sailor, home from the sea,
>   And the hunter home from the hill."
>   —Robert Louis Stevenson, "Requiem"

Tusitala's Road

Remembering the great love of his highness, Tusitala, and his loving care when we were in prison and sore distressed, we have prepared him an enduring present, this road which we have dug for ever.

These are the words the ten native Samoan chieftains inscribed on the marker for the new road from Stevenson's house to the main road when their labor was done.

The thick jungle growth had yielded slowly to the tools of the native workers, but the job was a labor of love. They called it the Road of the Loving Heart and proudly turned it over to the gentle Scot they had named Tusitala. He had come there at the age of forty suffering from a chronic illness; and although he gained strength in the mild climate, he was destined to live only four more years.

He loved to pass the time in the quiet of his home and study, yet he gave all too freely of himself in ministering to the needs of the islanders and their leaders. Many times he was called to spend long, arduous hours at the peace table settling disputes among the tribes. Again and again he visited rebel chieftains in the prisons, often interceding for them.

The day came finally in 1894 when the great soul left its frail body, and the chieftains bore him sadly to the peak of Vaea, his final resting place. The name they had given him, Tusitala, meant "teller of tales," for they knew that in the world from which he had come, he was a famous writer. But for them he was a special instrument of peace and loving compassion. Tusitala's "other world" still treasures his works—and still treasures the name of a wonderfully kind and gifted man: Robert Louis Balfour Stevenson.

These lines by William Blake (1785) might also have served as an epitaph:

> And all must love the human form
>   In heathen, Turk, or Jew;
> Where Mercy, Love, and Pity dwell,
>   There God is dwelling too.

"God whispers to us in our pleasures, speaks in our conscience, but shouts in our pains; it is his megaphone to rouse a deaf world."
—C. S. Lewis

THE PORTRAIT

Father Damien

The portrait of a grotesquely disfigured priest's face was more than the sensitive passersby could stand, and many stopped at the local art shop that morning to demand the repulsive object be removed from the window. They came out of the store in silence, many in tears, and some of them joined a line of those who stood waiting to purchase a copy of the painting. The reason for this sudden turn of heart was the realization that the man in the picture was Joseph de Veuster (1840–1889). Born in Belgium in 1840, he felt called to the religious life at eighteen, and taking the name of Father Damien he went to the Hawaiian Islands at twenty-three as a Roman Catholic missionary priest. He had no great intellectual talents, but he had one great gift—what some poets might call a touch of divine madness—a gift that led him to offer himself at thirty-one to the outcast sufferers living in the lonely leper colony on the island of Molokai.

When he arrived there he found that the sickness which was destroying their bodies had eaten away at their souls. A crudely inscribed sign declared, "In this place there is no law," although no sign was needed to advertise their gross, nearly depraved way of life. But Father Damien had brought his own law: God's love. He tended the sick, buried the dead, fed those who could not feed themselves, improved their pathetic homes and water supply systems, led their worship, and exhorted them to the godly life. His persistence made some turn against him, but the day came after ten years when he began his sermon with the words, "We lepers . . ." and his flock knew then he would ultimately give his life. He lived and worked for sixteen years more with the disease ever worsening.

His portrait was painted in later years and taken to England along with his story. The whole civilized world responded to the heroic sacrifice with prayerful admiration, and many could see in that ugly, loathsome countenance the ultimate beauty of life.

"The good God knows best what is good for my sanctification," said Father Damien, "and I say gladly, with ready heart, 'Thy will be done.' As for me, I make myself a leper that I may gain souls for Jesus Christ."

The machinery for declaring Father Damien a saint in the Roman Catholic Church is in fast-forward motion.

Some years ago a leper colony was visited by a U.S. Army officer who watched with dismay while an American nun dressed the sores of a leper. He turned pale and declared that he would not do the job for a thousand dollars. "Well," she responded, "I wouldn't do it for ten thousand," and, holding out her crucifix, she added, "but I would do it for Him."

What makes these people tick? Perhaps there is a clue in these words of poet Edwin Arlington Robinson: "There are two kinds of gratitude—the sudden kind we feel for what we take, and the larger kind for what we give."

HOW THE WILD IRISH ROSE

Turning the Tides of Fortune

The judge's angry, reddening face contrasted strangely with the powdered white wig that sat a trifle askew on his head that day in court many years ago in England. During the just concluded trial of the nine young Irish political prisoners who now stood before him for sentencing, he had struggled to control his temper in the face of their arrogant defiance. The judge took some comfort from the fact that they had been duly convicted of high treason against the queen, and he would silence their sassy mouths forever with the reading of the death sentence. "Have you anything to say," he inquired, "before sentence is passed?"

One of the lads, Thomas Meagher by name, had plenty to say: "My lord, this is our first offense, but not our last. If you will be easy with us this once, we promise on our word as gentlemen to try to do better the next time. And the next time, sure we won't be fools enough to get caught." The judge answered this outburst with a sharp rap of the gavel and ordered them off to the hangman.

The trial, which followed the Young Ireland disorders of 1848, had attracted world attention; and before the sentence could be carried out, pleas for mercy came to Queen Victoria from every corner of the earth. In the face of this pressure she commuted the sentence to life imprisonment in the faraway penal colonies of Australia. There were many who failed to see any real mercy in the change of sentence because Australia was then a savage land, and the ruggedness of life in some of the prisons was beyond imagination. But the commutation served to quiet most of the outcry, and the trial was soon forgotten.

It would have remained so, but in 1871 Queen Victoria learned that a certain Sir Charles Duffy had been elected Prime Minister of the state of Victoria, in Australia, and she was surprised to find that he was one of the nine men who had been convicted of treason years before. In searching the records of the other men, this is what she discovered: Thomas Meagher, the spokesman, had served as governor of the Territory of Montana in the United States. Terence McManus and Patrick Donahue were brigadier generals in the U.S. Army. Morris Lyene and Michael Ireland had served, in turn, as Attorneys General of Australia. John Mitchell was an important New York politician (his son was later elected mayor), Richard O'Gorman was Governor General of Newfoundland, and Thomas McGee had been President of the Council for the Dominion of Canada.

The pleas for mercy that turned the tides of fortune for the young Irishmen may have seemed small things to the individuals who made them, but in their total effect they were strong enough to change the mind of a queen, they overruled the decision of a stern court, and they allowed the pages of history to be brightened with nine distinguished records of service. Sure and begorra, this is more than the "luck of the Irish."

George Bernard Shaw once declared that his tailor was the only man who really behaved sensibly. "My tailor," he said, "takes my measure anew every time he sees me, whilst all the rest go on with their old measurements, and expect them to fit me."

THE PHILOSOPHER'S TOUCHSTONE

William James

I t wasn't so much that he wanted to die. It was just that there
seemed to be no other daring and manly way for a Harvard
man to gain freedom from the unbearable spiritual and physical misery from which he suffered. Born into a brilliant and
wealthy family, the son of a famed theologian, he had in his thirty-
eight years managed to achieve varying degrees of failure in the
pursuit of art, science, medicine, and teaching, and he had worried away his once perfect health in the process.

What little pleasure the distressed young Harvard instructor
had these days came from reading; and on that particular afternoon in the year 1880 he was sitting in his room at Cambridge
scanning a philosophical essay by Charles Bernard Renouvier. He
found free will defined in the essay as "the sustaining of a thought
because one actively chooses to sustain it rather than any other
thought." The sentence embedded itself in his mind, and he suddenly realized that for him it could be the passkey out of the prison
of sickness, frustration, and unfulfillment. Reaching for his note-
book, he wrote, "My first act of free will shall be to *believe* in free
will. I will . . . voluntarily cultivate the feeling of moral freedom
. . . . I will go a step further with my will, not only act with it but
believe as well—believe in my individual reality and creative
power."

That he opened the wellspring of his creative power that day is
not to be doubted. There was a new vigor in his teaching, his health
returned, and his interests broadened. Within a few years he had
written pioneering books in the fields of psychology and philosophy and had become one of the intellectual leaders of his day. The

still highly controversial philosophy of pragmatism he came to expound had a profound effect on religion, education, sociology, and politics in his day, and his "moment of truth" that afternoon will color life in America and the world for years to come.

We do not know whether further generations will admire his particular philosophy, but they will surely join with Dr. Joseph Fort Newton in this tribute to the personal victory of the great American philosopher William James (1842–1910):

> My old teacher, William James, was one of the happiest men that ever lived. He was so full of life, so eager, so optimistic, so sure of himself, so radiant, so high-spirited. All of us thought it was his temperament, so gay and gallant. He must have been born that way, we said. But no. It was a victory won, an art mastered, a task attempted and a job done.

The sovereign cure for worry is prayer.—William James

William James once interrupted a confused student who was holding forth tiresomely on the subject of Mind and Matter. "What is Mind?" queried James, and then added quickly, "Never mind, what is Matter?—no matter, never mind."

THE LAST HERETIC

Pierre Teilhard de Chardin

Pierre Teilhard de Chardin (1881–1955) may come to be remembered as one of Roman Catholicism's last notable heretics—not because there will be no more greatly respected yet maverick minds (like Hans Küng or Matthew Fox) traveling along the farthest edge of theological propriety, but because church authorities are beginning to show more and more reluctance to apply the term to the many bright, adventuring minds that are to be found today in that communion. The why of the matter is not hard to understand: any scholar whose ways of life and thought earn great respect outside the Roman Catholic Church ought to have at least a measure of acceptance within his or her own religious community.

Teilhard was born and raised in Auvergne, France. A Jesuit, he studied extensively in the fields of physics, chemistry, geology, and paleontology, and he achieved a reputation as an explorer as well. He was a volunteer stretcher-bearer in World War I and following the war lived for many years in China and other parts of Asia. Toward the end of his career, while living in New York, the sometimes whimsical, sometimes headstrong Teilhard was ordered by church authorities to stop his activities, and at the time of his death he was considered to be something of an outcast from Jesuit ranks.

Sir Julian Huxley, biologist, assesses the importance of Teilhard's work in a comment that appears in a publication of the American Teilhard de Chardin Association of New York: "Once he had grasped and faced the fact of man as an evolutionary phenomenon, the way was open towards a new and comprehensive system of thought. It remained to draw the fullest conclusions from this central concept of man as the spearhead of evolution on earth, and to follow out the implications of this approach in as many fields as possible. . . . In my view he achieved a remarkable success, and opened up vast territories of thought to further exploration and detailed mapping."

The association's document goes on to explain that in Teilhard's system of thought "the origin and development of both man and the universe must be understood in terms of a continuing evolutionary process. The world and man as they exist today are but one stage in an unfinished process of completion (which will continue until a new and higher level of consciousness, self-awareness and self-understanding is achieved—the 'biological perfection' of man)." Not unexpectedly, the diversity and scope of his writings have engendered controversy. Teilhard is now a voice of the past speaking to the future. Scholars of many fields are impressed and intrigued by his attempt to fit varied scientific disciplines into one vision of reality. His work is the subject of seminars and symposia all over the world. And so—if the term "heretic" does indeed fall out of use, it will be history's way of paying homage to the brilliant Jesuit, and many others like him, for a sincere, disciplined, and reverent pursuit of truth.

Faith has need of the whole truth.

Some day, after mastering the winds, the waves, the tides, and gravity, we shall harness the energies of love, and then, for the second time in history, man will discover fire.
—Pierre Teilhard de Chardin

PART V

Today's Roll Call of Honor

HELEN KELLER'S THREE LIVES

Helen Keller and Annie Sullivan

It is not given to everyone in this life, as it was with Helen Keller, to live three lives: in infancy as a normal baby, in childhood as (in her own words) a "half-animal," and in adulthood as one endowed—so most of us believe—with nearly superhuman qualities of perceptiveness and sensitivity.

Helen Adams Keller (1880–1968) was born in Tuscumbia, Alabama, a sound and healthy child. At nineteen months she was stricken with a fever that resulted in the total and permanent loss of sight and hearing. Her speech, which had barely begun to develop, soon lapsed into meaningless grunts and shouts. During the following years of early childhood, her frustration, arising out of her inability to speak or communicate, caused her to become ill-tempered and unmanageable. She would often throw herself to the ground in hysterical fits of anger, rolling and screaming until she lay exhausted. Her eating habits were less tidy than most animals, and she allowed herself to be taught only the most minimal practices of self-care.

When she was seven, a miracle took place—a wonderfully gifted teacher, Anne Sullivan (1866–1936), came into her life. Miss Keller's own words tell the story: "Reason hardly warranted Anne Sullivan's attempt to transform a little half-human, half-animal, deaf-blind child into a complete being. Neither science nor philosophy could set such a goal, but faith, the eye of love, did. I did not know I had a soul. Then the God in a wise heart drew me out of nothingness with cords of human love and the life belt of language and lo! I found myself."

The account of how Helen Keller reached the point of spiritual development and maturity where she could speak in such a manner is a story unto itself. Early efforts at religious instruction were a disaster—the pious assertion that God created people out of dust had sent the youngster into gales of laughter. After only a little discussion the family decided to seek the advice of a kindly clergyman, Dr. Phillips Brooks. The distinguished Episcopal rector thought hard and long about the way in which he might best introduce religious ideas to her. Anne Sullivan had told him of her concern at the failure of Helen's aunt to convey essential matters of faith to the child. And she had been worried, moreover, about the attempts of a rather strange psychologist to persuade the youngster's parents to keep her completely shut off from all outside ideas about religion so that they could make "valuable contributions to psychology" as they watched religious concepts "develop by themselves" within the walled-off mind.

The idea of permitting their daughter to be used as this kind of guinea pig did not seem to bother her parents much, but Miss Sullivan knew that the young soul could not be starved into development. Her own attempts at religious instruction had begun with discussions of Mother Nature and had ended abruptly with the little girl's innocent and direct questions about "Father Nature."

Dr. Brooks began to speak to Helen of God as the great and loving Creator-Father, and of men as brothers bound together in their love for him. As he spoke, the tutor, Anne Sullivan, "translated" his beautifully simple thoughts by "writing" on the palm of the pupil's hand—a method of communication by touch she had taught her years earlier.

The whole world now knows the importance of that day in the life of Helen Keller. Her richly developed spirit is an inspiration to all who have known or heard of her. She would have come to full bloom, perhaps, whether she had known Dr. Brooks or not, and, certainly, she received wise religious counsel from others. But it is a matter of history that the clergyman-poet (he wrote the words to "O Little Town of Bethlehem") was there to help at that crucial time more than one hundred years ago, and the guidance he gave her then supported her—as it will indeed support anyone who has "ears to hear." "And so," he told her, "love is everything—

and if anybody asks you, or if you ask yourself what God is, answer, 'God is love.' "

The story of Helen Keller's subsequent incredible growth in mind and spirit is familiar to millions. At twenty-four, with Annie Sullivan as constant companion and "interpreter," she was graduated with honors from Radcliffe College. She regained her ability to speak after years of mammoth effort, and she blossomed fully as a lecturer. She became a fine writer, and showed remarkable perceptiveness in philosophy and religion.

But most important, she developed completely as a human being—loving and loved—and it is for this that she has become the symbol of courageous hope, not only for the disabled but for everyone who treasures the thought that the human spirit is capable of infinite growth and progress. After the "three lives" I noted earlier, Miss Keller saw a fourth: "I look forward to the world to come where all physical limitations will drop from me like shackles, where I shall again find my beloved Teacher [Annie, who died in 1936], and engage joyously in greater service than I have yet known."

When we are born of the flesh, we are utterly helpless and dependent, while in the spiritual birth we are active, and in a sense creators. We have nothing to do with our birth into existence; for we must exist before we can make anything of ourselves. On the other hand, our birth into life is a matter of choice, we have a very direct share in it; for no real spiritual life can be thrust upon us against our will.—Helen Keller

Many people marvel when I tell them I am happy. They imagine that my limitations weigh heavily upon my spirit. Yet, it seems to me that happiness has very little to do with the senses. If we make up our minds that this is a drab and purposeless universe, it will be that. On the other hand, if we believe that the world is ours, that the sun and moon hang in the sky for our delight, there will be joy.—Helen Keller

I do not want the peace which passeth understanding; I want the understanding which bringeth peace.—Helen Keller

IN MEMORIAM: MARGARET SANGER

Leaders of many countries even today still resist the birth planning ideas of America's Margaret Sanger. It's fair to say that they are engaged in a very tough battle—if the history of the Planned Parenthood movement in the United States is in any way indicative of what may be happening in other parts of the world.

In 1912 when Margaret Sanger (1883–1966) was a young nurse working in the New York slums, she became enraged at the pain, misery and death of women who suffered after self-induced abortions or who were forced to go to a crude and filthy five-dollar abortionist to have the illegal operation performed. Even when pregnancy and delivery were normal, Sanger saw the tragedy of unwanted children and worn-out mothers. In desperation she wrote a pamphlet titled *Family Limitation*, in which she described then-known contraceptive methods. For her efforts she was nearly jailed, because legal definitions of the time classified such information as "lewd and obscene literature." Four years later, in 1916 she founded a birth-control clinic in Brooklyn and was promptly jailed, although the thirty-day sentence was quickly reversed.

The story of her last fifty years is more familiar to us. Biographer Lawrence Lader sums it up in *Margaret Sanger and the Fight for Birth Control* (Doubleday, 1955):

The message that Margaret Sanger stamped ineradicably on her time was that human beings could consciously control the plan and purpose of their lives; that out of the evolutionary process they could raise society to a new level of dignity and beauty. . . . As a woman, Margaret Sanger glorified *love* as the most powerful force in our destinies. . . .

The social revolution she brought in her own country has been so sweeping and decisive in the space of a few decades that, paradoxically enough, many young mothers today take birth control as much for granted as if it were incorporated in the Bill of Rights. Yet in vast areas of the world the force of her revolution is only taking hold. . . .

Perhaps it was Margaret Sanger's genius that she could fuse such qualities as innocence and gentleness with her inexhaustible determination to give women the biological control of their lives.

THE ROLL OF HONOR

Ralph Bunche

The stunning victory of racial prejudice over the sensitive spirit of Ralph, an African American teenager, sitting in a Los Angeles high school classroom more than seventy years ago, was nearly complete as he struggled to control the overpowering flood of soul-consuming anger and humiliation he felt. His grades, the highest in his class, had earned for him the right of membership in the city-wide scholarship honor society; but the honor list had just been read, and his name was missing. The embarrassed glances of students and teachers told him the reason: color.

As he walked quickly out of the room, the intention to leave the school and forget all about graduation had already formed in his mind, but later when he had found a place of privacy and quiet he tried to think the matter through. His thoughts drifted back to a precious evening five years earlier when he had sat talking about hope and ambition with his mother. Although he had not realized it at the time, she was aware that death for her was not many months away, and she had tried to pass on to him a strong philosophy of life. She had said, "Never let anything take away your hope and faith and dreams." But how, he wondered bitterly, could hope survive in the face of cold, unreasoning bias?

It was a long time before a firm answer came, but it did come. The burdensome pressure of racial prejudice was outside his life, thought Ralph, and hope was within. Hope would not die so long as he had the will to preserve it, and this he determined to do. His courageous decision to go on with graduation and to hold on to hope at all costs has affected lives other than his own.

It was the spirit of this decision which carried the now-famous

American statesman, Ralph Bunche (1904–1971), to the position of United Nations Undersecretary General. It was his contagious spirit of hopefulness that led him on one occasion to effectively mediate a dispute between Jews and Arabs in Palestine, an achievement for which he was later awarded the 1950 Nobel Peace Prize. And it was this same spirit which was caught by his son, a seven-year-old polio victim, who came back to full health after a crippling attack of childhood's most feared disease.

The life of the former UN official was marked by many encounters with racial bias (while carrying out his duties in the high world office he was once refused service in a dining car that was traveling through one of the border Southern states), but in each encounter he showed the hopeful patience that won for him his own crucial battle against prejudice. Someday, that same spirit will drive this evil from our world.

> Whenever someone speaks with prejudice against a group—Catholics, Jews, Italians, Negroes—someone else usually comes up with a classic line of defense: "Look at Einstein!" "Look at Carver!" "Look at Toscanini!" So, of course, Catholics (or Jews or Italians or Negroes) must be all right. They mean well, these defenders. But their approach is wrong. It is even bad. What a minority group wants is not the right to have geniuses among them but the right to have fools and scoundrels without being condemned as a group.
>
> —Agnes Elizabeth Benedict

It really happened: U.S. Ambassador to the United Nations Warren Austin once urged the Arabs and Jews involved in the 1948 Israel crisis to get together and settle their problem "in a true Christian spirit." So much for diplomacy.

SONG OF THE DEEP RIVER

Marian Anderson

The solemn beauty of the Negro spiritual "Deep River" has touched and blessed the lives of people in many wonderful ways, but it had a particularly happy effect on the life of one of the world's greatest singers, contralto Marian Anderson, an African American. It happened this way: In 1924 when Miss Anderson was in her mid-teens, she went to a well-known vocal instructor, Professor Giuseppe Boghetti, to try to arrange for singing lessons. The busy teacher took one look at the strong-faced black girl and made an impatient gesture directing her to leave. When she refused to move, he declared, "Go away, I tell you!"

Words were not easy for the young woman at that moment. How could she possibly tell him about the long hours of hope and study and practice that had brought her to his doorstep? And how could she describe the sacrifices that had been made on her behalf? Her father, an ice-and-coal peddler in South Philadelphia, had seen and appreciated her obvious musical talents while she was still a very small child and had worked hard to save every penny possible to start her career. Mr. Anderson's untimely death had forced her mother to take employment as a cleaning woman in a department store, but because of her pitifully small salary she took in washing to help support the family. Marian and the other children helped with this, but they were not allowed to skimp on their studies in order to earn money for household expenses. Many people had been kind to her and had helped in various ways not only to encourage her singing but to give her modest financial support as well. Her voice, admired by all, was heard in many church choirs, and on special occasions in the community she was often asked to perform.

All this was in her mind as the professor's command was repeated: "Go away!" She did not move—and while the professor stood glowering she decided to speak to him in music. Without accompaniment, she began, softly, to sing "Deep River." The professor, surprised into silence by the marvelous tones, tried to retain his composure as a variety of emotions seemed to strike him all at once: admiration, disbelief, excitement, joy, humility. Minutes later he was able to ask, "Where did you get such a voice?" And she answered quietly, "From God."

A great career in music was born that day, and the "gift from God," as Miss Anderson then described her vocal talent, still belongs to the Giver. "You see, my friend," she would tell you, "my voice does not belong to me alone. I hold it only in trust to God, who gave it to me, that through it I might bring comfort and joy to many people."

When I sing I try to let the spirit within me find pure expression.—Marian Anderson (1902–1993)

THE CHAPLAINS OF HELL

If, after this mortal life, you should be so unfortunate as to find yourself trudging along the burning streets of hell, don't be surprised if you see a Roman Catholic priest directing a volunteer fire-hose brigade from heaven. The priest, Father Joseph Timothy O'Callahan, gained his experience as a fireman during World War II when he served as a chaplain aboard the USS *Franklin*, an aircraft carrier. The vessel was struck by a five-hundred pound enemy bomb that set off a chain of gasoline and ammunition explosions inside the ship. Bursts of flame four hundred feet high shot through the upper decks, and the shop's steel deck plating buckled in the intense heat. Dozens of bombs, loose from their storage racks, rolled aimlessly about on the decks, ready to explode from the heat. Burning gasoline flowed around machine-gun belts, causing them to go off like strings of deadly firecrackers. Father O'Callahan, after participating in the rescue of trapped and wounded men in the lower decks, made his way topside and began to man a fire hose. The sight of the chaplain in his battle helmet with its white-painted cross, working among the hot bombs, inspired the exhausted and wounded crewmen to make a mighty effort to save the ship. And they did.

You will find other chaplains carrying on their ministries in hell. Dominic Ternan will be there, kneeling protectively over the suffering just as he did on earth when he was killed while using his body as a protective shield against enemy fire. You will see two Protestants, George L. Fox and Clark V. Poling, side by side with Alexander D. Goode, a Jew, and John P. Washington, a Roman Catholic. These four men, having given their life jackets to soldiers who had lost their own during the confusion and panic of a midnight torpedoing in the North Atlantic, stood arm in arm on the deck of the transport *Dorchester*, praying together as it slid beneath the waves. As certainly as a just God lives in heaven their prayer will never cease—and where could it be more needed than in hell?

When we remember the lives of these and other heroic chaplains, our pious wish is that when they have finished their span of years (a few are still alive and with us) they will find eternal rest and peace. But that is our wish, not necessarily theirs. Life in hell can be no worse than that which they endured, willingly, on this earth. And if heaven becomes their portion, they will still prefer to be found in hell where the action is—trying to save that which is lost, protecting men's souls in danger and torment, and giving their lives for their friends. Greater love hath no man . . .

VETERANS DAY ON OKINAWA

The long silver threads of the tracer bullets that awesome night during World War II seemed to tie the bombarding American warships to the shores of Okinawa. Gunnery Officer Bill Heffner, although convinced of the terrible necessity of his job, trembled as he watched the vast destruction. It was strange, he thought, that an old desire to dedicate himself to the ministry had been reasserting itself strongly during these last few days. Suddenly, as if there had never been any doubt, he knew what he would do when the war ended. Meanwhile, on the island itself, huddled in a deep slit in the ground, a Japanese foot soldier named Luke dug and scratched at the earth beneath him for another precious inch of safety. His thoughts at that precise moment, as he was to discover in conversations years later with Bill, were bringing him to an identical decision.

After the miracle of survival, both men honored their decision to sacrifice as much for peace as they had for war. Both enrolled in Episcopal theological seminaries and entered the ministry. Both chose the missionary field as their lifework, and both men—still unknown to each other—volunteered to help in the spiritual reconstruction of the island. It was there that Luke and Bill met for the first time. It was there they discovered, in the course of a long conversation, that they made their life-changing decisions at precisely the same moment. William Heffner became the administrator of the extensive Episcopal work on the island. Luke Kimoto was given charge of the large Okinawa colony for lepers.

THE UNWORTHY SPEECH

Abraham Lincoln and the Gettysburg Address

Many listeners felt that the speech was over before it had really begun, and as the speaker returned to his seat on the platform they looked questioningly at others nearby. Some were lifting their hands slowly, preparing to join in the light applause; a few sat with arms tightly folded in contemptuous silence; and still others appeared to be lost in their deep thoughts.

The gaunt, gray-haired speaker was only half aware of their curiously diverse reactions, for he was struggling to interpret something that was going on in his own mind and spirit. Shortly before delivering the military cemetery dedication speech he had been strangely moved to insert the phrase "under God" into one of the sentences of the oration he had written—but that was not all. The heartbreaking sight of the long rows of grave-markers stabbing, so it seemed, into the protective earth, suddenly etched into his mind a sharper understanding of the sacrificing Christ the crosses symbolized.

Later, in describing this experience, the man who had always been religious and who became all the more deeply so during his latter years declared, "When I left Springfield, I asked the people to pray for me. I was not a Christian. When I buried my son, the severest trial of my life, I was not a Christian. But when I went to Gettysburg, and saw the graves of thousands of our soldiers, I then and there consecrated myself to Christ."

In reporting the dedication ceremony, newspapers the next day showed a considerable range of opinion about the speech. Some took the view that it was totally unworthy of one in so high an office; others described it as profound, simple, and of great beauty.

The "totally unworthy" speech, Lincoln's Gettysburg Address, is now a part of the imperishable literature of freedom.

The Gettysburg Address

Fourscore and seven years ago our fathers brought forth upon this continent a new nation, conceived in liberty, and dedicated to the proposition that all men are created equal.

Now we are engaged in a great civil war, testing whether that nation, or any nation so conceived and so dedicated, can long endure. We are met on a great battlefield of that war. We have come to dedicate a portion of that field as a final resting-place for those who here gave their lives that that nation might live. It is altogether fitting and proper that we should do this.

But in a larger sense we cannot dedicate, we cannot consecrate, we cannot hallow this ground. The brave men, living and dead, who struggled here, have consecrated it far above our power to add or detract. The world will little note nor long remember what we say here, but it can never forget what they did here. It is for us, the living, rather, to be dedicated here to the unfinished work which they who fought here have thus far so nobly advanced. It is rather for us to be here dedicated to the great task remaining before us: that from these honored dead we take increased devotion to that cause for which they gave the last full measure of devotion; that we here highly resolve that these dead shall not have died in vain; that this nation, under God, shall have a new birth of freedom; and that government of the people, by the people, and for the people, shall not perish from the earth.

The phrase, "of the people, by the people, and for the people," was written by John Wycliffe in England in 1382 as a part of the preface to his translation of the Bible. This is what he said: "The Bible is for the government of the people, by the people, and for the people."

THE BABE'S MAIN EVENT

"Babe" Didrickson Zaharias

Most women athletes would consider winning Olympic gold medals as the greatest accomplishment of their careers. For Mildred Ella "Babe" Didrickson Zaharias (1914–1956) they were symbols of preparation for the greatest contest of her life. Cancer made the difference. Babe was never lacking in any of the feminine traits, but even as a little girl she could play baseball and basketball better than any kid on the block. When the 1932 Olympics were held in Los Angeles, and, after winning events in five tryouts for the American team, she astounded the sports world by winning the 80-meter hurdles and the javelin throw, and taking second place in the high jump. Later she turned to amateur golf and won all the important women's tournaments.

In 1953, five years after turning professional, she was preparing for competition in the all-important U.S. Women's Open when the blow fell—she learned that she had cancer. The operation called for was a colostomy, and on the night before it was scheduled she lay frightened and distraught on her hospital bed in Beaumont, Texas, convinced that she would never again play golf or lead a halfway normal kind of life. Her husband, George Zaharias, a one-time wrestler, and a good one, found himself with the gift of words as he sat beside her: "You were born to be a champion, Babe. . . . This is the main event. . . . Somehow you've been picked by the Almighty to win this fight, and when you win it people all over the world will take heart and lose some of their fear of cancer." George's thoughts, whispered close, gave Babe faith—and she relaxed and slept.

Successful surgery was only half the battle. During the long convalescence her wise nurse, Sister Marie Daniels, suggested that she would have less time to worry and think about herself if she did something to help those in the hospital who were much sicker than she. Babe and a friend, Betty Dodd, began to make regular visits to the various wards, cheering others (including a desperately ill nun); and in the course of the visits Babe remarked that her "spiritual muscle" was getting stronger.

The operation took place in April. In July the incomparable Babe walked away from the Salem Country Club at Peabody, Massachusetts, the winner of the U.S. Women's Open Championship by twelve strokes. Some years later death finally claimed Mildred Zaharias, but it didn't claim a loser. She had met the finest athletic competition of the world and won; and in the "main event" she had fought the bitterest fears of life and won. Her strength of body nearly matched her strength of soul. Faith made the difference.

POINTS OF LIGHT:
THE GREAT INVOCATION

Words of Wisdom and Inspiration

From the point of Light within the Mind of God
Let light stream forth into the minds of men.
Let Light descend on Earth.

From the point of Love within the Heart of God
Let love stream forth into the hearts of men.
May Christ return to Earth.

From the centre where the Will of God is known
Let purpose guide the little wills of men—
The purpose which the Master knows and serves.

From the centre which we will call the race of men
Let the Plan of Love and Light work out
And may it seal the door where evil dwells.

Let Light and Love and Power restore the Plan on Earth.

This is the United Nations Prayer. Circulated widely in the early 1960s, it may be the source of the "points of light" reference in George Bush's 1989 Presidential Inauguration Address. The phrase "points of light" is to be found in *The Magician's Nephew*, written by C. S. Lewis in 1955, and in Thomas Wolfe's *The Web and the Rock* in 1939. The phrase is also found in the 1945 writings of Alice Bailey, who recorded comments of a Tibetan monk, Djwhal Kuhl.

A meditation

O God, I stand before Thee, knowing all my deficiencies, and overwhelmed by Thy greatness and majesty. But Thou hast commanded me to pray to Thee, and hast suffered me to offer

homage to Thy exalted Name according to the measure of my knowledge, and to lay my supplications at Thy feet. Thou knowest best what is for my good. If I recite my wants, it is not to remind Thee of them but only so that I may understand better how great is my dependence upon Thee. If, then, I ask Thee for the things that make not for my well-being, it is because I am ignorant: Thy choice is better than mine, and I submit myself to Thine unalterable decrees and Thy supreme direction. O Lord, my heart is not haughty, nor mine eyes lofty, neither do I exercise myself in matters that are too great and too wonderful for me. Surely I have stilled and quieted my soul like a child with his mother; like a child is my soul within me!
—Bachya Ibn Pakuda, Hebrew philosopher, eleventh century

At dawning

Almighty God, who hast planted the Day-star in the heavens, and, scattering the night, dost restore morning to the world; fill us, we beseech Thee, with Thy mercy, so that, Thou being our Enlightener, all the darkness of our sins may be dispersed, through our Lord Jesus Christ. Amen.—Sarum Breviary, 1085

Praise note

Blessed art Thou, O Lord our God, King of the universe, who formest light and createst all things; who givest light in mercy to the earth and to those who live thereon, and in goodness renewest every day continually the work of creation. Selah. Blessed art Thou, O Lord, who formest the luminaries. Amen.—Early Hebrew prayer

In the morning

O thou who sendest forth the light, createst the morning, and makest the sun to shine on the good and the evil; enlighten the blindness of our minds with the knowledge of the truth; lift up the light of thy countenance upon us, that in thy light we may see light, and at last, in the light of grace, the light of glory. Amen.—Bishop Lancelot Andrewes, seventeenth century

Epilogue

Among the many short and simple parting benedictions, our family favorite is the single word, "Mizpah," taken from Genesis 31:49. We use the word itself to convey the benediction drawn from the verse (KJV):

> The LORD watch between me and thee,
> when we are absent one from another.
>
> MIZPAH

INDEX